Self-Esteem

and the

Social You

Anita Canfield

Special Thanks To
Tauna Lowe
Laurie Hightower
Ellen Christensen
Cover Photo Models

© Copyright 1982 by Anita Canfield
All rights reserved
ISBN: 0-934126-26-7
First Printing, October 1982
Second Printing, March 1983

Raymont Publishers
Orem, Utah 84057

ontents

Preface

As you read this book, leave your earthly roles in the other room. From cover to cover we are simply WOMEN, DAUGHTERS OF GOD, and SISTERS to each other. There will be a few references to mortal roles; that is necessary when we deal with self-esteem and the *social* you. This book is meant to help you understand what it is you feel that diminishes your self-esteem and how to correct that inadequacy.

It is so important as you read that you spend time reading and pondering *every* scripture given. If you do not, you will miss the real power of the message on these pages.

I hope you have read the other two books to this series. They were written in the order they came to me, both practically and spiritually.

Each is meant to introduce you to the next level of gaining self-esteem. The message in each is "part of the whole."

It has been said, "If you could catch the vision of the Woman God intends for you to become, you would rise up and never be the same again."

It is my desire that in these pages you will catch that vision; that you will read this with the spirit in which it was written; and when you are finished, that you will rise up and never be the same again.

With love,

ANITA CANFIELD

Chapter  One

The Power Within You

"A journey of a thousand miles must begin with one step."
—Chinese Proverb

Over the past two years since you and I have shared ideas, I have received a few thousand letters. These have helped me so much in knowing where to focus thoughts and concepts. And they have brought me to a more intense depth of feeling that our meeting is a "reunion." I am convinced that we knew one another and were more than acquaintances in our former life; we *felt* like sisters. I am also convinced that we wanted to help one another on this side of the veil . . . we really loved each other that much. This book is going to talk about those relationships and how they affect our self-esteem.

Now don't be misled. This book is still a book about only YOU and YOUR self-esteem. But when I refer to the Social You, it is *you* and how you feel about yourself, in relationship to those people and circumstances around you. It is a journey we will take together, because you and I are on the same road. We are mortal women working out salvation and exaltation.

Very often in life we find ourselves standing in the shadow created by the light of those around us or our own personal "social status." Consider some of the following circumstances that can cause feelings of low self-esteem. You are or are experiencing:

Single
Never married
Divorced
Widowed
Unhappily married
Married to an inactive member
Married to a non-member
Married without children
Married with many children
Overweight
Low income
No obvious talents
Lack of recognition for work performed
Weak family structure
Unrighteous dominion from a close priesthood authority
Lack of outstanding physical beauty
Inability to communicate

Can you identify with any of those areas? Do you answer "yes" to any of the following:

1. Making friends is hard for me.
2. I am unhappy.
3. I feel afraid.
4. I avoid competition.
5. When I feel criticized, I get defensive.
6. I feel inadequate.
7. When others succeed or gain praise, I feel inferior.
8. I rarely compliment others.
9. I am insecure about voicing an opinion or presenting my own ideas.

If you answer "yes" to even one of those statements, then you are experiencing weak areas in your self-image. You are experiencing *fears, doubts,* or *jealousy* and maybe all three.

It is *fear, doubt,* or *jealousy* that cause us to stumble while on our journey to renewed self-vision. Because we stumble frequently, the journey sometimes seems endless. But the proverb reminds us:

"A journey of a thousand miles must begin with one step."

1. That first step on the journey to a better self-image socially is to be able to IDENTIFY what you are feeling that is negative (fear, doubt, jealousy) and be HONEST about it.

It is often a painful step to take, to face yourself and admit that you have fear, doubt, or jealousy. But it is that first and VITAL step, and you will experience no progress until you begin to take it.

As I have read the letters that have come to me, some have cost me several hours of emotional energy. These are the ones that reflect a totally "I can't" attitude. One woman who visited with me reflected the theme of those letters. She was experiencing negative feelings but had not identified them yet.

She told me that she was single, never married, and felt guilty about that (fear). She said that she was totally unhappy and couldn't communicate with others or voice her opinion (doubts). She also said that there were people in her life who just did everything to gain praise for themselves and didn't care about her (jealousy).

Her self-esteem was suffering *socially*, and she wasn't "in touch" with her feelings. She was experiencing all three of those self-defeating attitudes and didn't realize it. For every negative feeling we have, there is a label. It will fall under one of the three: fear, doubt, jealousy. Look at the list again:

1. Making friends is hard for me . . . . fear
2. I am unhappy . . . . doubt
3. I feel afraid. . . . . fear
4. I avoid competition. . . . . doubt
5. When I feel criticized, I get defensive. . . . . fear
6. I feel inadequate. . . . . doubt

7. When others succeed or gain praise, I feel
   inferior . . . . jealousy
8. I rarely compliment others . . . . jealousy
9. I am insecure about voicing an opinion or
   presenting my own ideas . . . . doubt

To identify reaction and cause in your behavior requires being perfectly honest with yourself. It means getting control of emotions and thoughts. It means FACING yourself. It means not allowing yourself to rationalize or excuse away your negative behavior. Look at your behavior. If you find the negative, write down WHY you feel that way. Be honest.

As I watch my children experience the emotions of new circumstances, I see how easily they are affected by fear, self-doubt, and jealousy. As we get older, we become skilled in hiding from ourselves WHAT we are feeling. I think part of that is because we just don't realize WHAT we are feeling. Those negative reactions we experienced as children were never identified and so we have "grown up" with them.

When my daughter wanted to run for school vice-president, the entire family joined in and gave support. Steve made beautiful posters and had stickers printed with "Don't vote rashly—Vote Ashley." I helped her take them to school and helped her write her campaign speech (and listened as she practiced it). Her brothers helped her pass out stickers and chanted her slogan day and night.

Several days before the campaign speeches, Ashley tearfully announced she wanted to withdraw. She didn't think she could be vice-president. There were several running against her that were popular and she felt would win. All the standing on my head and praising her and telling her she had a good chance to win wouldn't comfort her.

Then it dawned on me. She was afraid to give her speech in front of the whole school. So I slowly began to ask her pertinent questions that forced her to *identify* what she was feeling—fear. That gave us something to deal with. Until then even she didn't realize what was happening.

Then we discussed fear. Yes, everyone is afraid of those kinds of moments. I let her know that sometimes when I have to give a talk, I am afraid, too. We talked about what we were afraid of. Things like: others might laugh at me, or not like my ideas, or think I look funny, etc., etc. There are some things we have to do even when we are afraid, but the more we believe in ourselves the less afraid we feel.

This talk changed her completely. It was what she needed to hear and deal with. We prepared her for the speech. All the candidates would give their speech on the school's closed circuit television. We practiced with that idea in front of a pretend camera.

On the day of the speeches, the television camera broke. All the students (over 500) were filed into the cafeteria. The candidates would be giving their speeches live! Ashley was unprepared for this, but she knew she had to do it. She didn't want to, but she went to the podium and began her speech. Tears filled her eyes, and she trembled, but she made herself do it. As she went to her seat, the entire school gave a tremendous cheer and a standing ovation. She won the election by a landslide!

Her self-confidence and self-esteem has really blossomed this past year. And I know it is because she identified a negative behavior, and that allowed her some growth.

When Steve and I see our children doubt themselves or show jealousy, we try to immediately make them identify WHAT they are feeling. Then we can discuss possible WHYS and begin the road to self-improvement.

1. The first step then is IDENTIFY WHAT you are feeling (fear, doubt, jealousy) and be honest about it.
2. The second step is to realize you have *within you* the *Power* to change those negative feelings.

Let's go back to the sister who came to visit me. She went on to tell me how she had read everything on the subject of self-esteem and self-mastery, literally dozens of books. She said there were great ideas and profound thoughts in all that material, but her self-esteem was still suffering. She stated, "I know the gospel is true. I know I'm a child of God, His daughter. I know the things I'm supposed to do, but I can't. I've tried, but I just don't have the *power* to change it. I want to, but the *power* isn't in me."

Parley P. Pratt said, "An intelligent being, in the image of God, possesses *every* organ, attribute, sense, sympathy, affection that is possessed by God himself." (*Key to the Science of Theology,* page 100)

Within each of us lies *power*, great power. So great a power that we can become like God. We are like our Father and Mother in heaven because we are literally Theirs. We belong to Them. We have inherited ALL Their organs and attributes and qualities, including the power to sublimate all those elements into Godhood. I testify to you it is as real a POWER as any kind of power you can describe now on this earth. It comes from DIVINE HEREDITY. We have inherited this from our Heavenly Parents.

Why do we, if this is true then, lose perspective and begin to feel powerLESS? Let me suggest some reasons:

1. I believe in that garden scene, as Satan was being cast out and was threatening to possess the bodies of Adam's posterity, that he was given a power over us. The POWER to BRUISE our heels, a very real POWER. It has a terrific force upon us, because the tool of his power is through our own thoughts! He can suggest to our mind, "You aren't capable," "You aren't worthy," "You've sinned one too many times." Or how about this one: "Everyone at church has her life in order but you!"

2. We see the woman we really are and the one we can become. The real versus the ideal. You have had that experience of success in one area, haven't you? For example, you are patient for one full day! You have tasted success; you KNOW you are capable of overcoming impatience. And then the next day you slip. You have caught a glimpse of the woman you can become,

the ideal. But you live daily with the woman you really are. The gap seems immense. The two can become closer at times but never seem to meet. It is good to be aware of that gap because it inspires us to be better. But it can also be discouraging. And then remember, who is the Father of Discouragement?

3. We live daily with our weaknesses and inadequacies, but we don't allow others to see them. We try to hide them from the view of others, right? I certainly don't want anyone observing me losing my temper or being impatient with my children. We cover up our inadequacies by putting our positive side forward. There is nothing wrong with accentuating the positive. The problem is, we forget that everyone else is doing the same thing! Then we truly respond when Satan whispers, "See, I am right! Everyone does have their life in order but you!"

4. We feel we will never measure up to the Mormon Mold image. We seem to be going in different directions all at once. We succumb to the pressure of being cook, seamstress, laundress, nurse, taxi driver, chairman, Good Samaritan, etc., etc., etc. We sense we are jack-of-all-trades, master-of-none — it is called "feeling fragmented." Somehow we perceive the ideal LDS woman as being married to at *least* a stake president, mother of five, pregnant with number six, gourmet cook, perfect seamstress who always arrives looking like an 8×10 glossy, state fair award winning breadmaker, makes her family's entire wardrobe (including the bedding and draperies), teaches Gospel Doctrine, a true scriptorian, supplements the family income by running a successful cosmetic business from the trunk of her car, and has her Christmas presents (all handmade) done by October.

These are very literal powers Satan has over us, but you can see how we help him along, especially when we compare ourselves to others.

But in that same garden scene I believe a loving father endowed us with a greater *power*—the *power* to crush Satan's head. It, too, is a real power—the power to win—the power to succeed—the power to become a God! The tool for us is the same as Satan's—the power to crush his head is also through our thoughts. "I am capable," "I am worthy," "The Lord does love me," "I can succeed!" We can say to ourselves: "The gap between the real and ideal me is sometimes wide and sometimes narrow. That's okay. I'm grateful for the gap; it propels me to do better. I am grateful for my weaknesses; they WILL become my strengths. I will put on the WHOLE armour of God!"

"I will accentuate my positive side in an honest manner. Okay, I'm not perfect, but in some things I am or will be soon. I will be reasonable about my positive side and measure my success with only myself."

"It is a worthy goal to seek perfection, especially in specific areas. I will continue to do so. But I will not become pressed with the feeling of failure because I hate baking bread, or I am not married, childless, married to an inactive man, etc. I am wonderfully UNIQUE. There is no one like me. I can and must be a success by being ME!"

If you have never considered such thoughts as POWER, you have been missing part of the greatest gift you have ever been given. The *power* through your own thoughts.

3. The third step is realizing you are UNIQUE and truly special and have a great mission here on earth.

Ask yourself a most profound question: "What are the two most important days in my life." (It is with inner power that you can know and understand the answer.)

THE DAY YOU WERE BORN.

THE DAY YOU REALIZE *WHY* YOU WERE BORN!

And why were you born? You were born to bless the lives of others. And how will you do that? You will do so by your UNIQUENESS, by your *differences*. We should be *cherishing* our differences by using the power you have been given, with which you have been endowed.

One day I was looking up a reference in *Mormon Doctrine* and I turned to a column titled "Straight and Narrow Path." The first sentence read, "The course leading to eternal life is both *strait* and *straight.*" (Emphasis added.) Now I found this most curious. In reading this particular verse in the scriptures and encountering both spellings of straight, I had always assumed it was just a misspelling or the way a translator had spelled it. It never, until that moment, occurred to me it might be intentional. Elder McConkie continued, "It is *straight* because it has an invariable direction—always the same. There are no diversions, crooked paths, or tangents leading to the kingdom of God. It is *strait* because it is narrow and restricted . . . *straightness* has reference to direction, *straitness* to width." (Emphasis added.)

This was mind expanding for me. Let's explore that idea just a step further, together.

I went to the dictionary and looked up the word *strait*. The first definition was, "A narrow space or passageway."

Near my husband's home in Seattle between the Canadian and United States border is a narrow passageway of water that connects the Pacific Ocean with the Puget Sound. It is called The Straits of Juan De Fuca. I know there are other straits you are familiar with, too. There are the Bering Straits, The Straits of Gibraltar, The Straits of Magellen. We only need explore a globe or world map to find others. Many wars have been fought to gain possession of a strait, because they are important passageways that link two bodies of water.

I found myself remembering the history of the ancient sea captains who entered those straits. Upon entering the strait, the captain himself would come to the helm. Each captain was responsible for seeing his ship safely through. Depending on his type of vessel, the currents, the winds, the time of year, the seasons, the climate, the time of day (so many variables), he would make *individual* and *unique* decisions as to guide his vessel safely through. His circumstances were *unique* to his vessel and moment.

Suddenly my mind expanded that scripture! New intensity came to its words. "Strait (Straight) is the way and narrow the gate, and *few* there be that find it." (Emphasis added.) I saw clearly a loving father who *cherished* my uniqueness and my ability to serve Him with my differences.

The strait we enter from the pre-existence to immortality is this life. We are the captains of our vessels. Each of us enters in different seasons, tides, circumstances. The narrow passageway goes in only one invariable direction. It is straight because there are no crooked paths or diversions leading to Eternal Life. The commandments of God are *straight*. But mortal life is your UNIQUE spirit and talents, and the way is a *strait* with individual width.

This concept of uniqueness came to me on another occasion many years ago as I finally, heavily burdened, went to the Lord about my goals and desires. As I hashed over some of the specifics about my talents, personality, and goals, I wondered (and felt guilty) about a seemingly contrary posture to others around me. Suddenly it became quite clear as I heard and sensed completely. "Anita this isn't baggage you picked up along the way . . . these are things you came with!"

You must stop smothering yourself (and others) with thoughts of sameness and mutual status. You must concentrate your energy on enhancing your own uniqueness and individuality. And you must do it with one purpose in mind—to help strengthen the Kingdom of God and BLESS THE LIVES OF OTHERS. These are things you came with!

4. The fourth step to renewed self-esteem is to MEASURE what success is for you.

It is a most difficult task to try to teach the TRUTH OF SUCCESS. What is success? How do you measure it? Are you a success? In the eyes of the world is it fame, fortune, achievement. And what is it in the eyes of the Lord? Do you want to be a success? Of course, you do! All of us want it. It is part of our innate sense of Godhood. He is a Success. But even though we know all that, our inner senses fear it; really we just fear failure.

Elder Boyd K. Packer put it this way:

> If one who is not well known and not well compensated claims that he has learned for himself that neither fame nor fortune are essential to success, we tend to reject his statement as self serving. What else could he say and not count himself as a failure? If someone who has a position of fame or fortune asserts that neither matters to success or happiness, we suspect that his expression is also self serving. Therefore, we will not accept as reliable authorities either those who have fame or fortune or those who have not. We question that either can be an objective witness.

So where does that leave us? What good is it to strengthen self-worth if we cannot define our success? What course is ours to pursue on the journey to personal success? How can we evaluate it fairly?

When we approach the thoughts of success, we compensate for our fears by doing what Elder Packer stated. Success for each of us has to be a personal and individual measure. We can't evaluate our personal progress or status by the merits and progress of others. It doesn't matter *where* you are, just so you are going in the right *direction,* with *lengthened stride.* That is a successful person! It is one who is taking all that they are, despite physical or environmental limitations, and making it more!

> . . . the Lord does not judge us by what we have but by what we do with what we have. The rich may be haughty, the poor envious, the powerful cruel, the weak sniveling. And those between the extremes may well be complacent and lukewarm . . .
>
> To be rich is good, if you can be humble.
>
> To be learned is good, if you can be wise.
>
> To be healthy is good, if you can be useful.
>
> To be beautiful is good if you can be gracious.
>
> There is, however, nothing inherently bad in being poor, unlettered, sickly, or plain.
>
> To be poor is good, if you can still be generous of spirit.

To be unschooled is good, if it motivates you to be curious.

To be sickly is good, if it helps you to have compassion.

To be plain is good, if it saves you from vanity.

(Camilla Kimball, *Ye Are Free To Choose,* pamphlet, page 18)

I can go down both lists and write in names of people who are rich, but humble; learned, but wise; healthy and always working for others; beautiful, but helping those around them to be beautiful, too; poor, but generous of spirit, always giving all they have; unschooled, but always learning something; sickly, but understanding of others and an example of courage; and plain, but confident and without guile.

As you ponder those statements, make your own list of those you know who fit the descriptions. It may surprise you to see those who are true successes. In the eyes of the world they may not be, but to the Lord and themselves they are! Another surprise will happen, too. You will see how your life is being blessed by *their differences!*

5. The fifth step is to discover where the TOOLS are that will help you in renewed self-esteem and how to use them.

Remember the woman who came to visit me? After she left, I wondered about the things she had said. I kept asking myself how she could feel so *powerLESS in the light of her testimony.* In the light of her knowledge, she felt *NO POWER,* no ability to succeed. The *power* is real, and was there, and I knew it. Convincing her would be necessary. But then I began to think where the tools to use that *power* come from. They come from the gospel of Jesus Christ. He gave us the tools by which we could unlock that power, and it is with that inner power that each woman will rise. Then I realized it is one thing to know the gospel is true and another to *know* the gospel.

> I'm impressed with the testimony of the man who can stand and say he knows the gospel is true, but what I would like to ask is, 'But, sir, do you know the gospel?' I say it is one thing to know the gospel is true and another to know what the gospel is. Mere testimony may be gained with but perfunctory knowledge of the church and its teachings as evidenced by the hundreds who are now coming into the church with but bare acquaintanceship. But, to retain testimony and to *be of service in building up the Lord's kingdom* requires a serious study of the gospel and a knowing of what it is. (Hugh B. Brown, emphasis added.)

How can we "be of service in building up the Lord's Kingdom" if we are spending huge amounts of emotional energy on our own well being and self-serving pursuits? I know and bear testimony that the Lord knew what would be required of us in building up His Kingdom. And so He provided the very tools for us to use within the framework of His gospel. The tools to eliminate *fear, doubt,* and *jealousy.* The mighty killers of self-esteem.

Success in self-esteem will be found in KNOWING and then LIVING the gospel of Jesus Christ.

If I were asked to describe the gospel of Jesus Christ in one sentence it would be this: The gospel of Jesus Christ is FAITH—HOPE—and CHARITY.

And I believe that the tools to self-esteem lie within that gospel and specifically what the gospel is, those three words:

FAITH   HOPE   CHARITY

> . . . but whether there be prophecies, they shall fail, whether there be tongues, they shall cease; whether there be knowledge, it shall vanish away.
>
> For we know in part; and we prophesy in part.
>
> But when that which is perfect is come, then that which is in part shall be done away . . .
>
> And now abideth faith, hope, charity, these three . . .
> (1 Corinthians 13:8-10, 13)

The apostle Paul made it clear that the day would come when spiritual gifts would cease. The gifts of prophesy, tongues, etc., would be enveloped in something greater. When "that which is perfect is come," or the "perfect day," we will know all things, and so those spiritual gifts won't be needed. However, Faith, Hope, and Charity will "abide" forever. Faith, which is the POWER of God; Hope, which is the expectation and assurance of eternal progression; and Charity, which is the pure love of Christ.

"Therefore O ye that embark in the service of God, see that ye serve him with all your heart, might, mind, and strength, that ye may stand blameless before God at the last day . . . and *faith, hope, charity* . . . qualify him for the work." (*Doctrine and Covenants* 4:2-5, emphasis added)

There lies in those three words the whole kit for self-esteem. Every tool you will need to put in motion your power within is contained in *Faith—Hope—*and *Charity.* The gospel of Jesus Christ is a gospel of:

Believing. . . . . Faith
Expectations . . . . Hope
Love . . . . Charity

The lack of faith is *fear.*
The lack of hope is *doubts.*
The lack of charity is *jealousy.*

The great prophet Moroni spent the entire seventh chapter of his book discussing *faith, hope,* and *charity.* It is a chapter all about self-esteem.

He showed us they are not only interrelated, they are interdependent! I believe that when you feel good about Heavenly Father and the Savior, you love Them and believe in Them and what They tell you (faith). When you feel good about yourself, you can love yourself and expect better for yourself (hope). And when you feel good about others, you can love and serve them (charity). There will be no fear (lack of faith), no doubts (lack of hope), and no jealousy (lack of charity). If you do not love God, you cannot love yourself or others. If you do not love yourself, you cannot love God or others. And if you do not love others, you do not love God or self. How you feel about others and treat them is how you feel about yourself. Faith, hope, and charity— not only interrelated but interdependent.

> Wherefore, if a man have faith he must needs have hope; for without faith there cannot be any hope.
>
> And again, behold I say unto you that he cannot have faith and hope, save he shall be meek, and lowly of heart.
>
> If so, his faith and hope is vain, for none is acceptable before God, save the meek and lowly in heart; and if a man be meek and lowly in heart, he must needs have charity; (Moroni 7:42-44)

I believe within these three words lie the keys to unlocking the power within you! In this book we will discover those keys.

6. The sixth step to finding self-esteem is to ACT.

In his instructions to women (DHC IV 602-607, DHC V 19-21), the Prophet Joseph Smith used the word ACT with firmness:

> ACT in the sphere allotted to you, filling the several offices to which you are appointed. ACT in the place appointed and thus be sanctified and purified. If you neglect the duties devolving upon you . . . you will be darkened in the mind . . . ACT in all things on a proper medium . . . for where there is a mountain top there is also a valley . . . You are now placed in a situation in which you can ACT according to those sympathies which God has planted in your bosom . . . You should aspire only to magnify your own office and calling . . . You are responsible for your own sins . . . If you depart from the Lord, you must fall . . . You are responsible to God for the manner you improve the light and wisdom *given by the Lord to enable you to save yourself.* It is a desirable honor that you should walk before your Heavenly Father as to save yourself. Said Jesus, 'Ye shall do the work which ye see me do.' These are the grand key words for you to ACT upon. (Emphasis added.)

The six steps again to gaining self-esteem socially are:
1. Identify what you are feeling that is negative (fear, doubt, jealousy) and be honest about it.
2. Realize you have within you the power to change those negative feelings.
3. Realize you are unique and truly special and have a great mission here on earth.
4. Measure what success is for you.
5. Discover where the tools are that will help you in renewed self-vision and how to use them.
6. ACT or in President Kimball's words, "DO IT NOW!"

It is my desire that in this book you will find the tools you need to improve your self-esteem socially. Steps one, two, three, four, and six will be aided as you concentrate on step five. It is my desire that you know how much I have grown to love you, that I feel this is a personal conversation between the "two" of us. I am writing to each one of you *individually.*

I want you to know that everything I write is based on personal testimony. I wouldn't write it if I had not found it to be true. It is impossible for me to write about things I have no feeling for. Therefore, you must be prepared for the very personal experiences I will share with you. I hope none will be offended. They will be my personal *learning* experiences. Notice I used the present tense, *learning.* I have not truly *learned* much yet. I am an ordinary woman, working out her salvation like everyone else. I am no different than you. If these things I am about to share with you have opened my understanding and are *working* for me, they will work for you. I promise you that.

What Joseph Smith instructed us to do is our DUTY. It is our DUTY to ourselves, our families, mankind, and to God. We cannot even doubt our responsibility in gaining self-esteem and self-mastery. And if it is our DUTY, then God has given us POWER TO DO IT! None of us could succeed at that council unless we had the POWER to do so!

Oliver Cowdry said, "Should you in the least degree come

short of your duty, great will be your condemnation, for the greater the calling, the greater the transgression." (*Doctrine and Covenants* 2:195)

You have and will have many great callings in mortality, but what greater calling is there than to develop yourself in such a manner that you can become as God is?

We were prepared in great eons of time for today and for that which lies ahead. Many of our ancestors and loved ones will rise up and call us blessed for all we will pass through. We are now living in a time to prepare ourselves. We had better know our duty.

I believe knowing our duty, having reason to succeed, and gaining self-esteem and self-mastery are clearly and carefully defined in the gospel of Jesus Christ. I believe the reason we are born is to bless lives, to be of service in building up the Lord's Kingdom. I believe we need to focus on developing faith, hope, and charity in order to succeed at self-esteem and self-mastery. And I *know* we have the power within us to do so.

So does the Lord: "It is not meet that I should command in all things . . . Verily I say, men should be anxiously engaged in a good cause, and do many things of their own free will, and bring to pass much righteousness; FOR THE POWER IS IN THEM . . ." (*Doctrine and Covenants* 58:26-28, emphasis added.)

Chapter  Two

Faith

"Every great enterprise begins with and takes its first forward step in faith."

—Schlegel

Faith is a word you have heard all of your life in the Church. There is a reason it is the first principle of the gospel. The same reason it is the *first tool* in gaining self-esteem. It stands at the doorway to accepting the gospel, and it stands at the doorway to accepting yourself and building self-esteem.

YOUR THOUGHTS ON FAITH CANNOT BE NEUTRAL!

You must "awake and arouse your faculties" regarding your understanding of how faith unlocks the power within you. Faith *is* power.

> . . . *faith* is the moving cause of *all* action . . . faith is not only the principle of action, but of *power* also . . . faith, then, is the first great governing principle which has *power* . . . over *all* things. (Joseph Smith, Lectures on Faith, emphasis added.)

The scriptures are laced with the declaration of faith as a principle of power and the primary key to the use of the power within each of us.

"Jesus said unto him, If thou canst believe, *all things* are possible to him that believeth." (Mark 9:23, emphasis added.)

"And neither at any time hath any wrought miracles until *after their faith*;" (Ether 12:18, emphasis added.)

"And Christ hath said: If ye will have faith in me *ye shall have power* to do whatsoever thing is expedient in me." (Moroni 7:33, emphasis added.)

"Remember that *without faith you can do nothing;* therefore ask in faith. Trifle not with these things; do not ask for that which you ought not." (*Doctrine and Covenants* 8:10, emphasis added.)

"Ye endeavored to believe that ye should receive the blessing which was offered unto you; but behold, verily I say unto you there were *fears* in your hearts, and verily *this is the reason that ye did not receive.*" (*Doctrine and Covenants* 67:3, emphasis added.)

Faith is based on truth and is preceded by knowledge. Until you gain a little knowledge of the truth you cannot have faith. You cannot believe in something that you know nothing about. How can you have faith in Christ if you've never heard of Him or do not *know* of Him?

"Faith is *not* to have a *perfect* knowledge of things; therefore if ye have faith ye hope for things which are not seen, which are true." (Alma 32:21, emphasis added.)

Faith is the believing in that which is not seen but is true. The synonym for *true* is *real.* Then faith is the believing in that which is not seen but is real. God is real, you are real, your ability to become like Him is real. You cannot see the woman God intends for you to become, but you have been taught the concept. The knowledge has been given to you that you are preparing now to become a queen, a priestess, a God. Therefore, it is up to you to have faith in that which is not seen but is true.

The knowledge of the Future You and your ability to be Her will be gained through the power of faith. YOU MUST BELIEVE IN WHO YOU ARE AND WHAT YOU CAN BECOME!

Having faith in yourself requires you to first have faith in God. How can you believe you are able to become like Him if He is not real to you? If He is real to you:

1. You understand His mind and intentions for you.
2. You believe what He has given you to overcome on this earth is for your own good.
3. You trust Him.
4. You love Him.
5. You have faith in Him.
6. You are able to feel His love in return.
7. That love inspires and encourages you.
8. You have faith in yourself because you can *feel* God's confidence, love, and support for you.

If you do not have faith in yourself, or enough faith in yourself, perhaps what you've been seeking isn't burning desire. Exercising enough faith helps us *prove to ourselves* that what we seek is truly a desire. If you aren't realizing your desires in self-improvement, you are not desiring in faith with all your heart! You are allowing yourself to be swallowed up by what you cannot see!

In order to develop faith and then increase it, there are some specific things you need to do:

1. Exercise self-control
2. Alter your thoughts
3. Gain knowledge
4. Seek spiritual gifts
5. Have courage

Exercise Self-Control

In developing or strengthening faith, it is vital to remember "the powers of heaven cannot be controlled nor handled only upon the principles of righteousness." (*Doctrine and Covenants* 121:36)

The power at your disposal is governed by law, the laws of righteousness, more specifically—personal righteousness. And that takes self-control. Self-control is the ability to carry out a commitment once the enthusiasm is gone. It is the spirit in control of the body.

When we commit to do something—lose weight, stop smoking, pray daily, keep a clean house, quit gossiping, or anything—in the beginning we feel such enthusiasm for our decision or commitment. Usually something or someone has inspired us to do it. We go home all enthused and vow to succeed! The first day, even the first week, are usually exciting as we anticipate progress and feel self-esteem. But before long, that effort we make becomes routine, and the zeal and fervor wanes as our effort turns to gut-level labor!

Personal righteousness doesn't mean that you are ready to be translated. It means that you are *striving* to be an obedient daughter to *all* the commandments of God. It means you are exercising self-control and are loyal to the commitments you have made in the gospel, marriage, motherhood, PTA, weight control, and whatever. Remember, it is not WHAT you do but HOW you do it! Perfection is a process, not an event!

Sister Kimball tells the following story:

> Many years ago, when we were vacationing in Long Beach, California, I went to the public library to look for books to read. As I browsed through the shelves, a strange woman came up beside me and with no preliminary introduction said to me in a demanding voice, 'Are you saved?' Taken aback, I paused a second to consider. Then I answered, 'Well, I'm working on it.' With firm conviction, she admonished, 'You'd better accept Christ now and be saved, or you may be too late!' I have thought about this encounter many times since, and my answer to the question would of necessity still be the same today: 'I'm working on it.' (*Blueprints for Living,* page 19)

Where do you begin working in order to gain self-control? If my spiritual progress seems to be in slow motion, or if I find self-control seems a struggle, I always find the reason in one place: BASICS. It is vital to get back to basics!

Are you having daily personal prayer (morning and evening)?
If you've been to the temple, do you attend regularly?
Are you reading the scriptures daily?
Are you attending all your meetings?
Do you repent daily?
Are you diligent in your church assignments?
Do you fast regularly?

Those are the basics. In order to feel any power at all in self-control and any effectiveness in personal righteousness, you have to get back to the basics.

Self-control helps us to build character. As we build character and see our influence in the world, we begin to develop more faith in our personal ability to succeed.

Karl G. Maeser was a most tender and spiritual man, and yet he was a strong spirit who stood up to be counted on the Lord's side. He demonstrated through his life how self-control shaped character. His influence was felt on the campus of Brigham Young University as he helped develop and establish that school. Now as the students go forth from that institution, his character is influencing the world!

> Brother Maeser, therefore, wisely made it his purpose to warm them spiritually; — to kindle in them the glow of enthusiasm, and trust the rest to self-effort. His teachings soon bore fruit in every town and hamlet in Zion, for God had prepared the people for his work, and given to Brother Maeser only the mission of supplying the leaven. Part of the educational ferment which immediately followed, is seen today in these splendid buildings, — so different from the early home of the Academy.
>
> But buildings and equipment are only a small part of the monument Brother Maeser has reared in Zion. If the greatest effects of his work be summed up in one word, that word would be —Character. He gave a new and fuller meaning to the qualities for which that word stands. Commercial integrity the world already had, — business relations can be relied upon to foster it; intellectual existence will ever make men keen and alert; but Brother

Maeser, while not neglecting these qualities, made higher requirements. He insisted upon physical integrity, the keeping of our bodies free from vice; upon social integrity, purity and chastity in the relations of the sexes; upon moral integrity, the doing to others as we would be done by; upon spiritual integrity, the anchoring of our souls in Heaven by a testimony of the Gospel. All these things enter into the new meaning of character. It is by such weapons the Latter-day Saints are to conquer the world. (Karl G. Maeser, page 149)

Adam S. Bennion, Superintendent of Church Schools, relates the following incident which he says was told to him by a man from Bear Lake County. This man said of himself that he was one of the roughest men in the whole valley.

With some companions I had been out riding horses all one Sunday afternoon, and we had planned to spend the evening together as we had been in the habit of doing. We used tobacco, and we used profanity, and we did the things that boys in a frontier country often do, which we knew we ought not to do. It was announced that one Karl G. Maeser was to speak in our Meeting House that night, and for some reason it got into my head that I would go, though the rest of the fellows would not. I did not know who Karl G. Maeser was, but I shall never forget him. I do not know what it was about him; I cannot tell you now — but when he was through talking I had been born anew; I will never forget that experience. When I went home, I said, 'Mother, you have a new boy!' and when she looked up in astonishment, I continued, 'I listened to Karl G. Maeser.'

Superintendent Bennion continues:

And he said from that night forward there had come into his life a force which had never been there before. He said he could not trace it to words; the language was not the thing, text was not the thing; but he said that he had felt that he had been in the company of a great character, and out of that company he came changed, with a new vision. He was actually remade. (Karl G. Maeser, pages 98-99)

Self-control helps us increase personal righteousness. Increased personal righteousness brings us closer to God. Drawing closer to God increases our understanding of His intentions for us and allows us to bask in His love. That is faith in Him.

Self-control also helps us to develop character. A good, strong, and righteous character increases our ability to succeed. A good, strong, righteous character helps us influence for good. That is faith in ourselves.

Elder Bruce R. McConkie said, *"Faith is a gift of God bestowed as a reward for personal righteousness.* It is always given when righteousness is present, and the greater the measure of obedience to God's laws the greater will be the *endowment* of faith." (*Mormon Doctrine,* page 264, emphasis added.)

Alter Your Thoughts

Self-control is altering your thoughts. The late Charles P. Steinmetz, famous engineer of the General Electric Company, a few months before his death (in 1945) stated: "The most important advance in the next fifty years will be in the realm of the spiritual — dealing with spirit — *thought*." (Emphasis added.)

The more scholars study thought, the more aware they are becoming of what a terrific force it is and how unlimited are its powers. Look around you. Everything that you can see has come from one source, that strange force called *thought.*

Your very life is your thinking and the result of your thought processes. You can physically be reduced to seventy percent water and a few minor chemicals of little value, but it is your spirit and mind and what you think that makes you what you are! History has left us with numerous accounts of how thought has made weak men strong and strong men weak. All the great religious leaders, kings, warriors, statesmen have understood thought power. They have known that people ACT AS THEY

THINK and also REACT to the thoughts of others, especially when it is more convincing and stronger than their own. For this reason, leaders with powerful dynamic thoughts have led multitudes by appealing to their minds, sometimes leading them to freedom, sometimes into slavery. There never has been a time when we should study our own thoughts more than now in these last days of earth. We should try to understand them and learn to use them to improve our position in life.

If you are buried in the mud of negative thinking, then you must STOP NOW those kinds of thoughts. They will only destroy you. If your mind is darkened by doubts, fears, worry about things unseen or undone, how can you achieve? If you are dwelling on the "lack of" in your life, you are slipping into a spiritual, social, and intellectual deformity. If you grovel in thoughts that *suppress* you instead of inspire you, you will never be anything more than a spiritual, social, and intellectual cripple.

A shoe manufacturer sought to expand his foreign market and so he dispatched two of his salesmen to similar primitive areas. Before long a cable came from the first: "Returning on the next plane. Impossible to sell shoes here. Everybody goes barefoot." Soon a cable followed from the second salesman: "Mailing fifty-three orders. Market possibilities unlimited. Everybody here goes barefoot." The attitude with which each salesman approached his assignment made the difference in his personal success.

Our life is what we make it by our own thoughts and deeds. It doesn't matter what your environment is or your physical limitations are; your world is what you make it. Your own thoughts, desires, and aspirations make for you a universe of beauty, joy, and bliss or one of ugliness, sorrow, and pain. By your own thoughts you create a heaven or a hell of life. As you build within the *power* of thought, so will your outward circumstances take shape accordingly!

Whatsoever you hold in the innermost chambers of your heart, no matter how hard you try to hide them from view, will eventually show itself in your outward behavior and circumstances.

My own little grandmother, Mamagrande, is an honor to her family and dearly beloved. She came from an environment that was a virtual breeding ground for negative thinking—she was poor, minority, and female.

Rafaela Garcia, at age thirteen, came to the United States with her mother and sister from Mexico after her father had been killed in the revolution. They came by mule over the mountains with no money and no personal belongings of any significance. They arrived in Texas, speaking no English.

Mostly because she knew her duty was to make her own way and to relieve the strain of "mouths to feed," she married my grandfather when she was sixteen.

During her married life, she lived most of it in extreme poverty. All of her children were born at home without help. For a time, she was a "servant" to her husband's family. She spent two years of her life living (with four babies) in a filthy border town where "the flies on the meat at the market made it look black." She reared her seven children in a two-room shack by the railroad tracks, with no indoor plumbing, sinks, or toilets, and an old coal-burning stove to heat the home and cook the food. My grandfather was a carpenter for the railroad and made $25.00 a month. They got their fresh vegetables by running after the produce trucks as they made their way to the Commission Road markets. The children gathered up whatever spilled off the back. They took turns buying clothes and shoes. If one needed new shoes and it wasn't his or her turn, they simply went without. One quart of milk was all they could afford for seven children for the whole week. Mamagrande had no education. She was not a member of the Church, but she believed that God would help her raise her children. She reared those children and taught them to believe in themselves. She could have said, "This is our lot in life. We live in the worst slums in Houston; there is nothing we can do. We haven't got a chance."

Instead, she taught her children self-reliance, the attitude of positive thinking, and that they must be the *best* they can be. She taught them by her example. Never complaining, never seeing the mud, only the stars, always being positive. She taught with impact.

My father was a straight "A" student in high school. In his junior year a teacher gave him a "B" on his report card, the first and only one he ever received. He went home with a heavy burden. He told his mother he knew he deserved an "A"; his work had been almost perfect. She told him to go back to the teacher and seek an explanation.

He approached his teacher with sincere bewilderment at receiving a "B" grade. It crushed his spirit as he felt the teacher's pure disgust when he replied, "Yes, your work was correct—but I'll never give a Mexican an 'A'!"

He could have returned to a home of mediocrity, negative thinking, and complacency—but he didn't. He returned to a home of excellence, positive thinking, and motivation! My little grandmother spiritually put her arms around her son's bruised self-esteem and taught him how great it was to be a Mexican! She taught him to *alter his thinking,* to *replace* self-doubt with thoughts of I CAN and I WILL! That experience could have been devastating for my dad, but instead it was turned into an experience to inspire him!

Out of her seven slum children came a retired army officer, a pharmacist-businessman, a chemical engineer, a scientist, a real estate tycoon, an artist-teacher, and a doctor. Two are millionaires, and the others are very comfortable financially.

My father told me that when he was nineteen years old, he went to war from that slum home. When he returned, after having exposure to the world, he only then realized how sad the living conditions were and helped his parents get out of there. But what he said revealed the mighty force of altering your thoughts to me: "Anita, we were poor, and we didn't even know it!"

I love Mamagrande for that. Today, in her humble way, she says she doesn't think she's done anything notable in her life. If you were to see her on the street, you would probably walk right by, seeing nothing more than a pint-sized, white-haired old woman with twisted, calloused hands. She never read Emerson's essay on self-reliance; she may not even know who he is. But she changed the course of generations of lives by her positive mental attitude.

When I went to Brigham Young University in 1964, I was sure I was going to be a fashion designer and enrolled in the courses of clothing and textiles and began my freshman year. As the months passed, I began to question that field for me. I spent time investigating what it would take to be a success as a fashion designer. The reality began to settle in past all the glamour—and besides, there were all those chemistry classes to take!

I found myself not really committed to clothing and textiles. I didn't feel at home with the outlined four-year course. I left school that June not knowing what I should do.

The summer passed, and I even considered not returning to BYU. A few weeks before I was to return, the new catalogue came. Now I know you will probably think this is a Mormon fish story, but it isn't. As I opened it, it literally fell open to two little pages marked "Interior Design." Somehow something inside of me recognized those words, and I *knew* that's what I should study. I really didn't know what it was. I didn't know you could go to college and study it. I read on. As I finished looking over the course material, a line from my patriarchal blessing came into my mind. It had been a long time since I'd read my blessing, so I went to dust if off and see if the sentence in my mind was there. It was. The very last sentence of the blessing said, "And you will be blessed to study those things in school and in the Church that will make you a useful woman for good."

From that moment on there was never a question in my mind that it was my duty to study interior design.

The day I graduated from BYU I held a dream. I wanted to

someday have my own business. The first client I had was a retired couple with unlimited funds. They had accumulated exquisite furnishings over the years and now wanted to "tie" it all together. We planned wallpapers, carpets, draperies, and a few additional pieces to blend. I was so excited. I could just picture the masterpiece it would be! Rich and dramatic, I knew it should be on the cover of *House Beautiful.*

The day it was finished I stood in the living room and felt completely diminished. It did not look like what I had thought it would. The clients wanted a muted, mundane background. They knew what they were getting after years of working with designers. I was the one who was surprised! They had more expertise than I did.

Even though it's what they wanted, inside I knew it lacked professionalism. It looked like any department store window. Where was the creativity, the genius, the pizazz? At that moment my faith weakened. I was overcome with fear. At that moment thoughts of owning my own business were gone.

I was fortunate to be working for a French woman who had lived nearly all her life in Paris. She taught me how exciting it could be to *break* the design rules I had learned in school. She taught me how to really picture the end result, and she taught me that creativity begins with vision.

I met another designer who shared ideas and desires. We agreed that we could make a great team. She had the business knowledge I lacked, and I had the design ability she lacked. We quit our jobs and formed our firm, each with an investment of $100. It looked as if my dream was coming true.

I was pregnant at the time with my second child. I took a leave of absence after six or seven months to have my baby. It was as if silence had fallen on the relationship between my partner and I. I didn't hear from her at all in more than six weeks. I called, but she was never there.

Three days after the baby was born, I called her. She was cold and indifferent. I said how excited I was to get back to work with her. She questioned my ability to do so. She said I couldn't possibly do it now with two children. She said I wouldn't be dependable anymore. I tried to convince her I could do it; I knew I could. She finally told me the truth—she didn't want a partner.

She wanted to "buy" me out. How could she pay for my gut level labor—and love of this field? I left with the $100 I came with, a little more, and a few samples. I also left with broken faith. Her parting words to me were doubts that I could ever make it as a designer.

I let her negative words and doubts creep into my own thinking. I guess it was over. I knew nothing about running a business. She didn't want me; maybe the clients didn't want me. I had two children. How could I possibly handle it all and be a good mother? I wasn't capable. I probably didn't have any talent either.

We needed money. My husband was still in school, so I went to work a few weeks later as a hostess in a pizza restaurant. I had made up my mind I would never be a designer again. Weeks passed. One day as I went inside the restaurant, into my mind came the thought, "What are you doing here? This is not what you prepared to do, Anita."

For the next few hours I wrestled between the negative thoughts of self-doubt and lack of faith (fear) and the positive thoughts of what I was capable of doing and my love for God and what I knew He had led me to study in school (faith). Slowly, and painfully, I began to *replace* those negative thoughts with the positive ones. I began to *alter my thinking*. It was done by *choice*. I had to work at it.

By closing time I went to the manager and gave him notice. The next day before work I went downtown and paid twenty dollars for a business license. I went over to the tax office and posted $30 for a tax number. Then I went to the bank with my remaining $80 and opened up a checking account under the name of Anita Brooks Interiors. I was in business with no samples, no clients, no money, and no real expertise at business. But I had regained the only asset I truly needed—faith. I knew I could do it if I worked hard enough. I was afraid. We needed money for school. I wanted to be a good mother, a full-time mother. But somehow, with faith enough, I knew I could do it all.

Over the next year I did $55,000 worth of business out of the trunk of my car and saved $10,000 of it. That was in 1974. The summer of that year my father's contract ended with the Atomic Energy Commission. He could see my enthusiasm and the potential in the business. He offered to be my partner and "open that little shop you've always wanted." I was thrilled!

We met obstacle after obstacle. We tried to borrow money, but money was not available. So we finally pooled resources, and each put in an equal amount and borrowed the rest against his house. I remember when we picked up the check. His house was his only investment at the time. If we failed, he could lose it, I thought. It was a negative thought. I expressed it to him, and what he replied in return has become our "motto." He said, "Anita, nothing ventured—nothing gained!" The old cliche has come to have real meaning for me. I looked at him and said, "Dad, I won't let you down. We can do it. I know we can make it!"

We made it.

In the beginning it was all for me. It was a step in a journey to a better self-image. It was and is very hard work to keep everything balanced evenly. I have made sure that I have been a full-time wife and mother, and that costs a heavy price. But the business has served a purpose. It has brought me, because of some lessons learned there, to a point that I am able to write to you today. Time and growth have changed, for me, the direction and course I must now go with it. But the message is: no matter *what* success is for each of us, no matter *where* success takes us individually, it all has its beginnings in ALTERING OUR THOUGHTS.

As you think, so will you be. Many people never grasp that because they can't see their mind as part of their spirit. Somehow they perceive a separation there. You cannot be separated from your thoughts.

Your being and mind is subject to change. You have the capacity for progress. Your being is changed by the thoughts you think. Herein lies the secrets of your destruction or your salvation and the secret is: MAKING THE RIGHT CHOICE OF THOUGHT!!!

Gain Knowledge

". . . to acquire faith men must gain the actual knowledge that the course of life which they pursue is according to the will of God . . ." (McConkie, *Mormon Doctrine,* page 264)

Faith can only develop and increase as we KNOW God. Joseph Smith taught that if we do not understand the character of God, we cannot comprehend ourselves. In other words, if we don't understand His mind and intentions, especially for us, how can we understand how He can expect so much from us or where we fit in?

God loves us all *alike,* saint or sinner, with a PERFECT and everlasting love. Maybe we don't always have His approval, but we always have His love. Perfect love is one hundred percent patience. That is why God can love us even though we sin over and over again.

His love for us is perfect. It is *our* love for Him that needs developing. We don't really mean we want to "build a better relationship" with Him, because the relationship of Father-daughter is already established. What we really mean is that we need to *draw closer* to Him. In drawing closer to Him you feel good about Him and love Him. That is developing faith. When we truly desire to please God, more than pleasing anyone else, even ourselves, then we can feel His approval and love surround us! These tender feelings make us feel our worth and His support. Our behavior changes and improves, and thus WE CAN HAVE

FAITH IN OURSELVES!

FAITH IN GOD = LOVE FOR HIM
TRUST IN HIM
OBEY HIS WILL

LOVE FOR HIM
TRUST IN HIM
OBEY HIS WILL = WE CAN FEEL HIS LOVE
AND SUPPORT TO US

We know that if we can *feel* that God knows we can succeed, we must be able to! You will know in your heart that He loves you, wants you to love yourself, wants you to succeed, and has definite intentions for you if you will pay the price to gain knowledge of Him.

"And this is *life eternal,* that they might *know* thee, the only true God, and Jesus Christ whom thou has sent." (John 17:3, emphasis added.)

Life eternal in this scripture means GOD'S LIFE, the kind of life He lives. To *KNOW* them means to become *LIKE* them, so we can have their kind of life. In becoming like them we will increase our faith in ourselves.

We can know God and the Savior by communicating *with* them. That is done through prayer and study.

1. PRAYER

We must understand that many prayers offered do not necessarily mean that communication has taken place. Prayer out of habit, or monologue, or without sincere intent are really in vain. When we get off our knees, there needs to be that "sweetness" present in our hearts.

Great promises have been given to us if we pray properly:

> If thou shalt ask, thou shalt receive revelation upon revelation, *knowledge* upon knowledge, that thou mayest know the mysteries and peaceable things—that which bringeth *joy,* that which bringeth *life eternal.* (*Doctrine and Covenants,* 42:61, emphasis added)

(Peace and joy are what you experience in the heart, and that is self-esteem.)

A.   When we pray, we should express deep gratitude and appreciation to Him for all we have and all we are. We should express love and devotion for each member of the Godhead. We should be most grateful for the Savior and for our knowledge of the gospel. Gratitude should be expressed for all the blessings, naming many of them, we have been given. In counting our blessings to the Lord we will lose sight of our problems. Counting blessings instead of troubles has always been a great comfort and counsel.

B.   We should be willing to conform to His will. We should be careful to ask only for those things that are right and tell Him "thy will be done." We must be *willing* to submit to His will and be obedient and accept the answer. If we are willing to accept the answer, then we will know we are humble—and we *will* be teachable. Obedience to God is Submission to His Will. If we are to end our prayers THY WILL BE DONE, why pray? In *Highest In Us,* Truman Madsen writes:

> As for 'thy will be done,' this, in the life of Joseph Smith as in the life of Christ, was not a turning *over* of all tasks to the Father *but a pulling of the Father's power into life.* Prayer was a leaf-by-leaf unfolding of potential, a recovery of their foreappointed mission. Likewise, the greatest prayer for us is a quest for the voluntary agreement, and in some ways an irreversible one, we made before mortality. Thus, 'Reveal me to me' should be as constant a prayer as 'Reveal thyself to me!' (Emphasis added.)

C.   "Reveal me to me" (reveal my weaknesses to me) will only be helped if we are openly honest in confessing our sins to Him. He already knows them. We can't try to cover up or hide our sins or shortcomings with fancy words or generalize them (please forgive me of my sins). We need to be specific! BEING HONEST WITH GOD IN OUR PRAYERS HELPS US TO BE MORE HONEST WITH OURSELVES!

D. We should seek the Spirit and ask for that companionship. If we are to find the things of the Spirit (FAITH, SELF-ESTEEM), we must search in the realm of the Spirit. To know *truth* by sense or feelings is possible by the Holy Ghost. It is necessary we pray for it and live worthy to have the companionship.

E. We should pray for our family, flocks, fields, friends, and enemies.

> Begin to exercise your faith unto repentance, that ye begin to call upon his holy name, that he would have mercy upon you;
>
> Yea, cry unto him for mercy; for he is mighty to save.
>
> Yea, humble yourselves, and continue in prayer unto him.
>
> Cry unto him when ye are in your fields, yea, over all your flocks.
>
> Cry unto him in your houses, yea, over all your household, both morning, mid-day, and evening.
>
> Yea, cry unto him against the power of your enemies.
>
> Yea, cry unto him against the devil, who is an enemy to all righteousness.
>
> Cry unto him over the crops of your fields, that ye may prosper in them.
>
> Cry over the flocks of your fields, that they may increase.
>
> But this is not all; ye must pour out your souls in your closets, and your secret places, and in your wilderness.
>
> Yea, and when you do not cry unto the Lord, let your hearts be full, drawn out in prayer unto him continually for your welfare, and also for the welfare of those who are around you. (Alma 34:17-27)

F. We should not become discouraged if our prayers at first do not seem inspired. We must grow to that point; it is part of being proven.

2. STUDY

"It's no longer a question of whether you have been through the standard works, but whether the life and light in them has somehow passed through the very skin of your bodies and enlivened you." (Madsen, *Highest In Us,* page 26)

Are you reading the scriptures daily? If you are not, you are missing personal words with God everyday. There is something eternal in those words to us. We have heard them before. They are familiar to us. As we read them, the veil thins, and we can sense where home really is. When we get that close to "home," we get closer to a glimpse of how great we really were before we came here! That feeling of greatness can linger with you all day.

In studying the scriptures, you can know the nature of God. You can "read His mind." It's great! You can begin to see the great plan for yourself—you begin to increase your faith in yourself!

"And as all have not faith, seek ye diligently and teach one another words of wisdom; yea, seek ye out of the best books words of wisdom; seek learning, even by study and also by faith." (*Doctrine and Covenants* 88:118)

"And set in order the churches, and study and learn, and become acquainted with all good books, and with languages, tongues, and people." (*Doctrine and Covenants* 90:15)

"And do thou grant, Holy Father, that all those who shall worship in this house may be taught words of wisdom out of the best books, and that they may seek learning even by study, and also by faith, as thou hast said;" (*Doctrine and Covenants* 109:14)

Notice how He clearly pointed out that strengthening faith is done by learning. If you diligently study out of the best books, including the scriptures, how does that strengthen your faith in yourself *directly?*

By increasing your knowledge, you feel more self-confident

in communicating with others. You feel more secure in your own opinion because you have studied enough to form credentialed opinions. A little knowledge can also decrease your feelings of inadequacy.

A friend of mine has a husband whose job requires him to travel. Several days before he was to leave on an extended business trip, their one and only car broke down in the middle of the grocery store parking lot. My friend calmly piled the children into the cart and went to the pay phone to call her husband to come and fix the car. Soon he arrived with a neighbor, and together they got the car started, and all were on their way again.

Car troubles were out of her mind until the day she dropped him off at the airport. On the drive home she began to really worry, "What if it stops again? I mean, what will I do? What if I have a flat tire? What if 'the this' and what if 'the that!'" As she rounded the corner by her house, suddenly she remembered the crash course she had taken in Relief Society. It was called Survival Mechanics. Sure, she thought, she could fix things, just to get by, just to get to a gas station or help. She had forgotten, because it was nice to depend on her husband. In her hour of need, she had felt inadequate.

Then hours later, thinking about fixing things enough to "just get by," she began to wonder about all the times she practiced Survival Mechanics—spiritually and intellectually. Learning enough to just get by does nothing to increase your self-confidence or self-respect. When you have paid a price to "seek learning, even by study and also by faith," you will feel more faith in your ability to voice an opinion or communicate with others. Your self-esteem will increase because your feelings of inadequacy will diminish.

Seek Spiritual Gifts

> Seek ye earnestly the best gifts
>
> For all have not every gift given unto them; for there are many gifts, and to every man is given a gift by the Spirit of God.
>
> To some is given one, and to some is given another, that all may be profited thereby. (*Doctrine and Covenants,* 46:8, 11-12)

Elder McConkie says that the purpose of spiritual gifts is ". . . to enlighten, encourage, and edify the faithful so that they will inherit *peace* in this life and be guided toward eternal life." (*Mormon Doctrine,* page 314, emphasis added)

Peace in this life can mean only one thing—peace of mind and heart, or in other words, self-esteem.

> Faithful persons are *expected* to seek the gifts of the spirit with all their hearts. They are to 'covet earnestly the best gifts' (1 Corinthians 12:31, emphasis added) . . . [referring to the *Doctrine and Covenants* 46, Elder McConkie continues] . . . we gain a clear knowledge of spiritual gifts and how they operate. Among others, we find the following gifts named either in these three places or elsewhere in the scriptures: the gift of knowing by revelation 'that Jesus Christ is the Son of God, and that he was crucified for the sins of the world' (*Doctrine and Covenants* 46:13), and also the gift of believing the testimony of those who have gained this revelation; the gifts of testimony, of knowing that the Book of Mormon is true, and of receiving revelations; the gifts of judgment, knowledge, and wisdom; of teaching, exhortation, and preaching; of teaching the word of wisdom and the word of knowledge; of declaring the gospel and of ministry; the gifts of faith, including power both to heal and to be healed; the gifts of healing, working of miracles, and prophesy; the viewing of visions, beholding of angels and ministering spirits, and the discerning of spirits; speaking with tongues, the interpretation of tongues, the interpretation of languages, and the gift of translation; the differences of administration in the Church and the diversities of operation of the Spirit; the gift of seership, . . .

And these are by no means all of the gifts. In the fullest
sense, they are infinite in number and endless in their
manifestations. (*Mormon Doctrine,* page 315)

It is significant the Lord said, "and to *every* man (and woman)
is given a gift . . ." It is up to you to read *Doctrine and Covenants*
Section 46 and ponder it in your heart. As you determine what
are your gifts, you should seek to strengthen them. If you don't
feel you have any, you should pray and study until you feel
familiar with seeking specific ones.

One spiritual gift we all should seek is teaching by the Spirit.
Teaching by the Spirit builds and strengthens faith. It also
strengthens those you teach. It is an eternal principle, when you
build and raise others, you build and raise yourself.

"The Spiritual gift to teach and influence by the spirit is
rightfully ours and will be ours as we desire it, *seek after it,* and
live to receive it. This blessing comes because of obedience and
personal righteousness, not because of administrative positions."
(Bruce R. McConkie, emphasis added)

I have heard it said that there are three kinds of teachers in the
Lord's Kingdom:

The Telestial—Those teachers who are condescending to their
students. They are well read and prepare with a dogmatic atti-
tude. They feel superior in knowledge and understanding to their
fellow members.

The Terrestrial—Also well prepared in content but they teach
to serve themselves. They leave a lesson feeling "I have done a
good job; I've done what I'm supposed to do. The Lord has to be
pleased with my performance."

The Celestial—These are they who teach because they love the
people they teach. They teach to change lives. They seek the
spirit in teaching. They leave a lesson hoping lives have moved
forward.

Our whole life is our preparation for teaching to change lives.
Our preparation is an on-going process as we pray, study the
gospel, and gain knowledge, as we gain experience through the

good and the hard times in our lives. The process begins with our own desire to learn! Over the years this will be used to bless other people and if we have paid heed and studied diligently, the spirit can draw to our minds things we have stored up and that now can be used to "bless others."

Heber J. Grant is said to have told the following story:

During a meeting in the Salt Lake Tabernacle he noticed his brother who had been very disinterested and indifferent to the Church, sitting in the audience. Elder Grant bowed his head and silently prayed that if he were requested to speak, he might have the spirit of revelation so that in some manner his brother would have to acknowledge to him that he spoke beyond his own natural ability and that he was, in fact, inspired of the Lord. Elder Grant said, 'I realized that if he made that confession, then I should be able to point out to him that God has given him a testimony of the divinity of this work.'

Elder Grant was invited to speak, which he did with great power. At the conclusion of his remarks, President Angus M. Cannon, who was conducting the meeting, called on George Q. Cannon to occupy the balance of the time. George Q. Cannon said he did not wish to speak. Brother Angus refused to take no for an answer. Finally, George Q. Cannon consented and went to the stand and said, in substance:

'There are times when the Lord Almighty inspires some speaker by the revelations of his spirit, and he is so abundantly blessed by the inspiration of the living God that it is a mistake for anybody else to speak following him, and one of those occasions has been today, and I desire that this meeting be dismissed without further remarks,' and he sat down.

Continuing his story, Heber J. Grant said, 'The next morning my brother came into my office and said, 'Heber, I was at a meeting yesterday and heard you preach.'

'I said, the first time you ever heard your brother preach, I guess.'

'Oh, no,' he said, 'I have heard you speak lots of

times.'

'I said, I never saw you in meeting before.'

'No,' he said, 'I generally come in late and go into the gallery. I often go out before the meeting is over. But you never spoke as you did yesterday. You spoke beyond your natural ability. You were inspired of the Lord.' The identical words I had uttered the day before, in my prayer to the Lord . . .

I asked, 'You know, what did I preach about yesterday?'

He replied, 'You know what you preached about.'

I said, 'Well, you tell me.'

'You preached upon the divine mission of the prophet Joseph Smith.'

I answered, 'And I was inspired beyond my natural ability; and I never spoke before—at any time you have heard me, as I spoke yesterday. Do you expect the Lord to get a club and knock you down? What more testimony do you want of the gospel of Jesus Christ than that a man speaks beyond his natural ability and under the inspiration of God, when he testifies of the divine mission of the Prophet Joseph?' The next sabbath he applied to me for baptism.'

Joseph Smith in *Instructions To Women* told us:

> *You are not to be ignorant of spiritual gifts.* You will receive instructions through the order of the Priesthood which God has established in this last dispensation. When your integrity has been tried and proved faithful, you will know how to ask the Lord and receive an answer. If you do right, there is no danger of your going too fast for God does not care how fast you run in the path of virtue.
>
> The devil has great power to deceive. The devil will so reform things as to make one gape at those who are doing the will of God. Be humble for you have a subtle devil to deal with, and he can only be curbed by humility.

In order to seek spiritual gifts, we must be humble. "Pride stand(s) as a bar to the receipt of spiritual gifts." (McConkie, *Mormon Doctrine,* page 370)

Some months ago a woman asked me, "How can you teach self-esteem when we are constantly being taught to be humble?" I looked at her for a moment totally empty of understanding her question. Then it dawned on me — she was equating self-esteem or love of self with a lack of humility! So I asked her, "Is Heavenly Father humble?"

After some discussion she concluded that yes, this omnipotent, all powerful, all knowing being is humble. The *quality* of humility is necessary to so be a God. But if we view God as an all knowledgeable, all creative, all powerful Being, we realize His self-acceptance (personal esteem) is also perfect. Then what is humility? Is it the antithesis of SELF-ESTEEM or self-love? How could it be if Heavenly Father is humble?

Humility is freedom from pride and arrogance. It is patience, long-suffering, submission, meekness, and lowliness . . . "and the remission of sins bringeth meekness and lowliness of heart . . ." (Moroni 8:26) In these words we find what is described as the accompanying virtues of humility . . . and yet . . . we must be careful here to clearly identify these very words. Too often, as the woman I mentioned, many are confused and have the idea that humility in its relationship to those words is a denial of self-worth.

If we consider the word "meekness," we often associate it with "weakness." We suggest that a meek person has no backbone, no voice, no strength. Therefore, if a person demonstrates qualities of strength or self-confidence (self-esteem), we place no value on their humility. Yet we know the Savior Himself talked about meekness as being a desirable quality. And yet He has admonished us to be strong and capable and cultivate self-respect through accomplishment. He was an extremely capable and powerful man—and yet, described as meek on so many occasions. I heard someone once describe meekness in an altogether different dimension for me. He said, ". . . meekness is *strength* turned *tender*." Now doesn't that expand that scripture more for you?

Let's consider "lowliness of heart." Have you ever felt guilty for being proud of an achievement or accomplishment? Have you ever been complimented and turned it aside with, "Oh, it was nothing." "I could have done better." "Really, this is just an old dress." It's almost like we are afraid to accept our strengths for fear we are saying that we aren't humble. "Lowliness of heart" implies groveling in feelings of "I'm really not much at all." We think if we aren't brooding on our weaknesses, we are not truly humble. And so, many are misled by semantics.

TRUE HUMILITY is the real appreciation of one's worth. It is self-acceptance. If you cannot *acknowledge your strengths,* you cannot *fully accept* your weaknesses (*accept* meaning understanding that they are for a purpose, by which to refine your spirit). How can you fully accept them if you cannot acknowledge your strengths? You would have no place to go and refuel your empty well. If you then cannot fully accept your weaknesses, you tend to not take responsibility for them or to blame them on someone or something else. Only when we fully accept our weaknesses can we change them; otherwise we just try to justify them.

TRUE HUMILITY is understanding that the Savior has justified each of us as a person of great worth. He suffered at Gethsemane and Calvary. He would not have done it if He had not believed we are worth that kind of sacrifice. We must understand we are worth the price He paid. WE ARE WORTH IT!

That thought overwhelms us with humility (or lowliness of heart. "I am worth the price He paid.") and gives us courage to accept our strengths—and then our weaknesses—forgive ourselves, love ourselves, and thus change. It is through love of self that change is initiated, and through that change we can overcome weakness, and that brings more love of self. May I share with you a letter from a sixteen-year-old girl who has learned TRUE HUMILITY:

> . . . I was born with a severe case of club feet. The
> doctors told my parents that if I hadn't been born today,

I would probably have never walked. I was put in casts up to my hips until I was six months old . . . When I was 11 I had a series of operations which gave me a permanent correction. I can remember so vividly laying in that hospital bed screaming in pain. I could not understand why I had to go through this experience; now I do. Through that experience I am able to empathize with people more and because of the severe pain and agony I became closer to Heavenly Father and learned the meaning of humility. At the end of my 11th year . . . my dad was called to be a mission president in Pennsylvania. I had always been an outgoing person and had lots of friends. I loved school and being involved. But when I moved to Pennsylvania, my new school had a full length mirror. For the first time in my life I watched myself walk in front of that mirror with other kids and realized that I was different. It wasn't a big difference, but I was rather deformed. As I walked in front of that mirror that difference became bigger and bigger. Everytime I saw myself I would get nauseated and feel a little dizzy. I would find other ways to get to classes even though it made me late. I began feeling sorry for other people who had to look at me. The outgoing person I once was became a bitter but quiet, timid person who was afraid to answer a question in class. I took it for granted everyone hated me as much as I hated myself . . .

She goes on to relate how she gained control of her life and attitude by altering her thoughts about herself, trying to succeed, and drawing closer to Father in Heaven through study and prayer. She concludes her letter with what she learned about humility:

. . . I have a close relationship with Heavenly Father— I became very close to Him since I followed the line of reasoning that if He created me, He was *stuck* with me (I can also help other people because of my relationship with Him.) . . . He created us and when we love and accept ourselves, we are telling Him that He did a good job!

True humility is when you are able to shed all your outer coverings, all your inner layers, and face the Lord totally "naked," totally honest with yourself and can still feel the love of the Lord for you. When you feel that love, you want to submit to His will.

Sometimes being humble and submitting ourselves to the will of the Lord is like eating a prickly pear cactus. We rebel at the thought of forgiving someone who has hurt us, or obeying a certain commandment, or following a leader who has hurt us, or following a leader who seems to be wrong, or as in President Kimball's circumstance, putting our infirmities on public display:

> In January he was assigned, with Elder Harold B. Lee, to divide the Dallas Stake and organize a Shreveport Stake. It was a hard week. He had a cold, diarrhea, two boils starting in his nostrils, some nosebleeds, and an excruciating back pain. Elder Lee, who shared his bedroom, asked him several times if there was anything he could do for him.
>
> After denying any difficulty until three in the morning, he decided that Elder Lee must know perfectly well from his twisting and turning that something was wrong. He then admitted he had been in constant pain for two days. Elder Lee gave him a blessing. Then Spencer slept a few hours, and the pain was gone and did not return. 'The Lord is so good to me and far beyond my deserts.'
>
> At the Houston conference Elder Lee, the senior of the two apostles, announced Elder Kimball as the next speaker. He stood, opened his mouth, but only an ugly grating noise came out. He swallowed and gulped and tried again, with the same sickening feeling. The thought came: 'Better quit—you can't do it—you can't impose on the people like this.' But he tried again, this time found his voice, and delivered his short sermon. Then he turned to Elder Lee, shrugged helplessly and sat down. Elder Lee put his hand on him and said, 'Thank you, Brother Kimball.'
>
> The next day there was another meeting in Houston. Elder Lee, in charge, announced Elder Kimball as the next speaker. He stood and 'made the most terrible sound you can imagine' until finally he found his voice and gave his

sermon. Then he sat down, buried his head in his hands and mourned. 'I was crying gallons of tears inside. I don't think they showed. But I really thought I was through, that I'd never preach again, that I wouldn't even try.'

Three days later, driving by car to Texarkana, he passed Elder Lee a note: 'I hope you won't embarrass me again.' Elder Lee jovially responded, 'Oh, I'm sure we'll call on you again. I think it's important for the people to hear your witness.' Elder Kimball answered nothing. He knew he would do anything Elder Lee, his senior, asked. *But inside he rebelled at the thought.*

The conference at Texarkana was held in a long, narrow Methodist chapel. True to his word, Elder Lee called on his companion apostle to speak. It seemed impossible. The public address system was out. The chapel was huge. Outside the window was the highway, with trucks climbing a hill, grinding and shifting gears. Elder Kimball stood and began, 'Brothers and Sisters . . .' He prayed silently, he strained, the words came. For ten minutes he bore his testimony. Every person in the chapel heard him. He sat down and Elder Lee put his arm around him and said, 'That's right, Spencer.' (*Spencer W. Kimball*, emphasis added)

What a tender example our beloved prophet shared with us on how being humble is shown through obedience to God. President Kimball has not allowed his pride to stand in the way of his spiritual gifts, for he has given the greatest of them.

Have Courage

Courage for what? Courage to have more faith! Maybe in the beginning it is easy to exercise even a particle of faith. In the beginning when hopes are high and you are determined to succeed, it's easy to have a little, maybe even a lot of faith. But when the going gets rough, when the answers don't seem to come, when our understanding is shallow, when we seem alone, then is it so easy to exercise faith?

"There are times when you simply have to righteously hang on and outlast the devil until his depressive spirit leaves you. While you are going through your trial, you can recall your past victories and count the blessings that you do have with a sure hope of greater ones to follow if you are faithful." (Ezra Taft Benson)

Being human we don't want to go through the trials but "after much tribulation come the blessings." (*Doctrine and Covenants* 58:4)

"And if thou shouldst be cast into the pit, or into the hands of murderers, and the sentence of death passed upon thee; if thou be cast into the deep; if the billowing surge conspire against thee; if fierce winds become thine enemy; if the heavens gather blackness, and all the elements combine to hedge up the way; and above all, if the very jaws of hell shall gape open the mouth wide after thee, know thou, my son, that all these things shall give thee experience, and shall be for thy good." (*Doctrine and Covenants* 122:7)

Our faith must be tried. We are proving to ourselves that we will be worthy of the callings to be assigned in another life. We must *earn* self-esteem here, not because Father has doubts about our competency, but because we need to grow and know we are capable to serve with full resources in the worlds to come. If you are not proven, you will *never be aware of all that you are!*

In his 1981 address at Women's Week, BYU President Jeffrey R. Holland asked the question:

> Over what issue or proposition was the War in Heaven fought?
>
> That is the whole exam. How did you do?
>
> Now I won't ask for a show of hands, but everyone who said 'free agency' or something like it—and I assume that is virtually everyone—has failed the exam. That is not the right answer. I gave you a one-question exam. Your whole future depended on it. Eternity was weighing in the balance. You've gone down the tube.
>
> Now before you slip out to the phone booth, call

Salt Lake, and have me working for the Methodists tomorrow, let me explain why free agency is not the right answer to that question. It isn't that it's wrong; it's just that it is not completely right. As I understand it, free agency was not the *original* issue over which the great War in Heaven was fought, regardless of what Sister Brown told you when you were a Merrie Miss. Certainly it did *become* an issue. That's why we have it as a theme today. That's why the scriptures are laden with the language. I am not denying the fact that it *became* part of the issue. I am just suggesting that some other proposition came earlier.

Now that I have made you sufficiently uneasy, I will ask the question again: If it is not free agency, then what was the issue over which the great premortal battle was fought?

May I suggest an answer? It was presented when God himself, our Eternal Father (and for all I know our Eternal Mother stood with him, though I know nothing of that, and we have nothing in the record) said to you and to me and to all others in our family, 'Do you want to be as we are?' I think that question started the War in Heaven. The issue was—and is—Godhood. Now incidental to that and almost instantly on the heels of it comes an issue like having free agency. You can't be exalted without exercising free agency. But when the discussion first began, I think the question from our heavenly parents was, 'Do you want to be as we are? Do you want to become gods and goddesses, kings and queens, priests and priestesses?' (*Ye Are Free to Choose,* page 4)

Before you and I came here, we wanted more than anything else to be like Father and Mother. We wanted that with all our heart and spirit! We lived with Them, we saw Them, They were a visual example to us. We wanted to become like Them.

We were willing to pay the price, no matter what it cost. We knew it would be worth it! It is not only worth waiting for, it is worth living for!

We were willing to pay the price *They* paid. How can we

become like Them if we don't go through what They went through to be where They are today? We were willing then to have our spirits taught and tempered in the refiner's fire, and we should be willing now. But being human we just don't want to suffer.

> No pain that we suffer, no trial that we experience is wasted. It ministers to our education, to the development of such qualities as patience, faith, fortitude and humility! All that we suffer and all that we endure, *especially when we endure it patiently,* builds up our characters, purifies our hearts, expands our souls, and makes us more tender and charitable, more worthy to be called the children of God. And it is through sorrow and suffering, toil and tribulation, *that we gain the education that we came here to acquire and which will make us more like our Father and Mother in Heaven!* (Orson F. Whitney, emphasis added)

Truman Madsen explained that one of the most misunderstood scriptures in Lehi's statement "Men are, that they might have joy."

> Christ came that suffering might result not only in good, but in its perfect work, which is perfection. He did not live to end all suffering, but to end all needless suffering and to turn suffering into joy, even in this world. (Latter-day Saints tend to ignore the context of the oft-quoted passage of Lehi's: '. . . Men are, that they might have joy.' 2 Nephi 2:25) Lehi teaches that joy could not arise except through contrasts of mortality. Mortal life is sweet, but it is bittersweet.
>
> The apparently, but not really, limitless mental and spiritual anguish that arises from life's buffetings takes on meaning. Pain becomes a laboratory of soul-nurture, and we may 'count it all joy.' The darkest abyss has its own revelations, its own chrysalis of higher promise. This is not myth! I testify it is the deepest secret of life. (Truman Madsen, *Eternal Man*)

It is a profound thought to me that WE MAY COUNT IT ALL JOY!

If all the skies were sunshine
Our faces would be fain
To feel once more upon them
The cooling splash of rain

If all the world were music
Our ears would often long
For one sweet strain of silence
To break the endless song.

If life were always merry
Our soul would seek relief
And rest from weary laughter
In the quiet arms of grief.

Henry Van Dyke

We came to mortal life to encounter resistance, and by doing so it will be our gain.

"Thou knowest the greatness of God, and he shall consecrate thine afflictions for thy gain." (2 Nephi 2:2)

Isn't that a tender word, *consecrate*? He really will do that for us. It makes tears come to my eyes when I picture an All Powerful God consecrating my afflictions for *my* gain. I love Him for that.

When resistence and opposition are strongest, our *faith, commitment,* and *personal growth* have the greatest opportunity for advancement. There is no other time that they do.

We cannot look back on Nauvoo, Kirtland, Jackson County, Clay County, Haun's Mill, Winter Quarters, and Deseret without realizing those names are synonymous with suffering. We cannot be exempt either.

"My son, peace be unto thy soul; thine adversity and thine afflictions shall be but a small moment;

"And then, if thou endure it well, God shall exalt thee on high; thou shalt triumph over all thy foes." (*Doctrine and Covenants* 121:7-8)

The Martin Handcart Company seemed to have been an ill fated group. Most of its members were convert immigrants from Europe who were too poor to buy oxen or horses or wagons. They were forced by their extreme poverty to pull handcarts containing what little belongings they had across the plains with their own physical strength.

A teacher, conducting a class, said it was unwise ever to attempt, even to permit them (the Martin Handcart Company) to come across the plains under such conditions.

Some sharp criticism of the Church and its leaders was being indulged in for permitting any company of converts to venture across the plains with no more supplies or protection than a handcart caravan afforded.

An old man in the corner sat silent and listened as long as he could stand it, then he arose and said things that no person who heard him will ever forget. His face was white with emotion, yet he spoke calmly, deliberately, but with great earnestness and sincerity.

In substance (he) said:

> I ask you to stop this criticism. You are discussing a matter you know nothing about. Cold historic facts mean nothing here, for they give no proper interpretation of the questions involved. Mistake to send the Handcart Company out so late in the season? Yes. But, I was in that company and my wife was in it and Sister Nellie Unthank whom you have cited was there, too. We suffered beyond anything you can imagine and many died of exposure and starvation, but did you ever hear a survivor of that company utter a word of criticism? Not one of that company ever apostatized or left the Church, because everyone of us came through with the absolute knowledge that God lives for we became acquainted with him in our extremities.

> I have pulled my handcart when I was so weak and weary from illness and lack of food that I could hardly put one foot in front of the other. I have looked ahead and seen a patch of sand or hill slope and I have said, 'I can

> go only that far and there I must give up, for I cannot
> pull the load through it.'

He continues:

> I have gone on to that sand and when I reached it,
> the cart began pushing me. I have looked back many times
> to see who was pushing my cart, but my eyes saw no one.
> I knew then that the angels of God were there.
>
> Was I sorry that I chose to come by handcart? No.
> Neither then or any minute of my life since. The price we
> paid to become acquainted with God was a privilege to
> pay, and I am thankful that I was privileged to come in the
> Martin Handcart Company. (Related by President David
> O. McKay)

To whom do we go when we suffer? We usually seek out
someone who has experienced a similar sorrow. When a patient
experiences a permanent illness or disability, the doctor has him
talk to another person with the same affirmity. There is strength
in that association.

When I was in labor with my first child, I wanted my
husband near, but I really wanted my mother there, too. She had
been through it; she knew what I was feeling. I knew she would
have compassion for me.

A wonderful friend of mine has a beautiful golden haired
toddler, one of the most lovely little boys I've ever seen. Without
warning he became gravely ill and was hospitalized for weeks.
There was talk of serious brain damage and other complications.
The parents were by his side constantly. They agonized over the
outcome for their beautiful child. They prayed and suffered and
prayed. They hung on to each other and drew closer as husband
and wife. But the time came when they both were suffering so
much, they could no longer help each other. At that point they
found what it meant to truly depend on and turn to the Lord.

He has suffered it *all*. He is the one person you can count on
for total compassion. When we become acquainted with him,
through our suffering, we know Him and can relate to Him. We
can receive a pure testimony, and nothing else in life will matter.

After World War II, Elder Ezra Taft Benson went to Europe to check on the condition of the saints. He tells this tender story:

> President Benson stood at the rear of the meeting-house and shook hands personally with each person present. Expressions of faith and devotion lighted their faces as they felt his warmth and sincere love for them. Some of these good people returned to the line a second and even a third time so that they might shake his hand again and be strengthened by his radiant spirit of love and compassion.
>
> While this was proceeding, President Zimmer pointed out to me a somewhat timid and emaciated sister. She had burlap sacks wrapped around her feet and legs in place of shoes. Even these were now in shreds. Her clothing was patched and tattered. As I looked at her purple-grey face, her swollen and red eyes, and protruding joints, I was told that I was looking at a person in the advanced stages of starvation. President Zimmer acquainted me with her hardships and incredible testimony.
>
> This good sister had lived in East Prussia. During the final days of the frightful battles in that area, her husband had been killed. She was left with four small children, one of them a babe in her arms. Under the agreements of the occupying military powers, she was one of 11 million Germans who was required to leave her homeland and all her basic possessions and go to Western Germany to seek a new home. She was permitted only to take such bare necessities, bedding, etc., as she could load into her small wooden-wheeled wagon—about sixty-five pounds in all—which she pulled across this desolate wasteland of war. Her smallest child she carried in her arms while the other small children did their best to walk beside her during this trek of over a thousand miles on foot.
>
> She started her journey in late summer. Having neither food nor money among her few possessions, she was forced to gather a daily subsistence from the fields and forests along the way. Constantly she was also faced with dangers from panicky refugees and marauding troops.
>
> Soon the snows came and temperatures dropped to about 40 below zero. One by one her children died,

either frozen to death or the victims of starvation, or both. She buried them in shallow graves by the roadside, using a tablespoon as a shovel. Finally, as she was reaching the end of her journey, her last child died in her arms. Her spoon was gone now, so she dug a grave in the frozen earth with her bare fingers.

As she was recalling these and other difficulties at a testimony meeting, she explained that her grief at that moment became unbearable. She was kneeling in the snow at the graveside of her last child. She had now lost her husband and all her children. She had given up all her earthly goods, her home, and even her homeland. She found herself among people whose condition resembled her own wretched state of affairs.

In this moment of deep sorrow and bewilderment, she felt her heart would break. In despair she contemplated how she might end her own life as so many of her fellow countrymen were doing. How easy it would be to jump off a nearby bridge, she thought, or to throw herself in front of an oncoming train!

Then she testified that as these thoughts assailed her, something within her said, 'Get down on your knees and pray.' And she then rapturously explained how she prayed more fervently than she had ever prayed before.

In conclusion, she bore a glorious testimony, stating that of all ailing people in her saddened land she was one of the happiest because she knew that God lived, that Jesus was the Christ, and that if she continued faithful and true to the end she would be saved in the Celestial Kingdom of God.

"Being human we would expel from our lives physical pain and mental anguish and assure ourselves of continual ease and comfort. But if we were to close the doors upon sorrow and distress, we might be excluding our greatest friends and benefactors. Suffering can make Saints of people, as they learn patience, long suffering, and *self-mastery*." (President Kimball, *Faith Precedes The Miracle*, 1972, page 98, emphasis added)

God will have a tried people!

Pain stayed so long, I said to him today;
'I will not have you with me anymore!'
I stamped my foot and said, 'Be on your way!' and paused
    there
Startled at the look he wore
'I, who have been your friend,' he said to me
'I, who have been your teacher—all you know of under-
    standing love, of sympathy, and patience—I have
    taught you. Shall I go?'

He spoke the truth, this strange unwelcome guest
I watched him leave and knew that he was wise
He left a heart grown tender in my breast
He left a far clear vision in my eyes.

I dried my tears and lifted up a song
Even for one who'd tortured me so long!
                              —Author Unknown

I received a letter from a sister who had experienced tre-
mendous adversity in her life. She had seen death, lost loved ones,
been abused, and her marriage had ended in divorce. She shared
heartbreaking experiences with me. As she concluded her letter,
she stated: "I have scars, physical and emotional scars. I am so
afraid they are there forever."

She need not wish for those scars to go. They are medals.
President Harold B. Lee once said: "We will not be judged by the
merits and badges we win on earth but by our scars. Do you catch
the significance of that?"

Sisters, catch the significance of that!

Over and over again I see a common question among those
who are suffering feelings of personal despair or weakness. That
question is: "Where is the Lord. Has he forgotten me?"

Sometime ago that question led me to believe that those
asking it were either not paying the price for the "guidance" or
else were in need of personal repentance. Although this is
probably the circumstance in many situations, it is not among the
majority of women who have written to me. Faithful, striving,

pure-in-heart sisters have expressed their inner feelings to me and shared some of their heavy trials, fully seeking answers, fully repentant and humble—and they asked that question.

It has caused me to reflect back on the many times in my life that I, too, have asked that question. One instance in particular comes to my mind. I had been suffering a tremendous burden for many, many months and had been pleading with the Lord for relief. It seemed finally as if the answer had come, but within weeks, it became very obvious that was not the answer or solution. Where was He! I asked Him over and over, "Where have YOU been all these months? Why have you forsaken me?"

As quickly as those words escaped my lips, several sentences entered my mind. I recalled a few paragraphs in Elder James Talmage's book *Jesus The Christ.*

Elder Talmage is discussing the great pain of Gethsemane, the trial, the mockery, the beatings and degradation, and finally, the agony of the cross and the heartbreak of rejection by those whom the Savior loved. He stated that even as half-God, the Savior could not have borne the process without the accompanying spirit of His Father. All along the way His Father's spirit was present, comforting, and strengthening Him.

Then Elder Talmage described such a beautiful truth, that if we truly understood it, our trials would become our jewels in merely moments. He said that the Father loved His Son so much, so dearly, that He wanted the Savior to *share* in the Glory! So for a few moments He withdrew His spirit, so that the Savior would be all alone—in His own glory. But so painful was it for Jesus that He cried out from the cross, "My God, My God! Why hast thou forsaken me?" And then He said, "It is finished" and gave up His life.

And so it is with our lives, our Heavenly Father loves us so much. He wants us to share in the glory, too. Consider the words of Truman Madsen: "That leads to the question of being 'guided in all things.' The diminuation or withdrawal of the Spirit — the dry spells and spiritual deserts we face are not always due to our unworthiness or to our failure. I am convinced they are part of our mortal trial and the will of the Lord. The Prophet Joseph had to cry out, 'O God, where art thou?' (*Doctrine and Covenants* 121:1) And the Master cried, 'Why hast thou forsaken me?' (Matthew 27:46) To that, one answer may be, 'Prove *yourself* devoted, even when I leave you in the realms of solitude.' This insight should not be distorted into the view, 'If the Lord has anything to say to me, I suppose He will.' If one goes along in indifference, neither seeking nor seeking to live worthy of seeking, he will not find." (*Highest in Us*)

I believe He loves us so much. He leaves us alone sometimes so that we may *prove to ourselves* that we can endure it. *Prove ourselves devoted* as Truman Madsen said. Can you imagine any greater joy than to meet Him face to face and be able to share in the Glory by saying, "I did it! I really did it! And now Father, I'm home . . ."

"Let us not presume that because the way is at times difficult and challenging, our Heavenly Father is not mindful of us. He is rubbing off the rough edges and sensitizing us for our great responsibilities ahead. May each of us follow the Lord's comforting counsel: "Be patient in afflictions, for thou shalt have many; but endure them, for lo, I am with thee, even unto the end of thy days." (*Doctrine and Covenants* 63:8, Elder James E. Faust)

The proving of our faith requires courage, "For after much tribulation come the blessings." (*Doctrine and Covenants* 58:4) Courage will strengthen our faith.

Exercising faith requires:
1. Self-control through personal righteousness
2. Altering your thoughts; as you think, so will you be
3. Gaining knowledge through study and prayer
4. Seeking spiritual gifts
5. Have courage to exercise more faith

"If ye will have *faith* . . . ye shall have *power* to do whatsoever thing is expedient in me . . . for it is by *faith* that miracles are wrought." (Mormon 7:33, 37, emphasis added)

"Remember, that without *faith* you can do nothing. . ." (*Doctrine and Covenants* 8:10, emphasis added)

Do you realize that virtually every good enterprise, great or small, that has ever materialized has stemmed from faith? The belief was that it could be done and that those people involved had the ability. Every successful business or corporation, every champion athlete, every new discovery or invention, every ambition realized, every celebrity or politician, every trip to the moon all happened because somewhere, someone had faith in themself and what they were doing.

Oh, if we could all have the perfect faith of a little child. One day this summer my five year old son was with me riding to the store. It was 115 degrees outside, a typical desert summer day. The air conditioner in the car was on full volume, but we were still sweltering. It had been a prolonged "heat wave" the weathermen were saying.

I looked at him and said, "It's so hot, isn't it? I wish it would cool down."

He replied, "It will, it's going to rain."

I looked up at the bright blue sky, not a cloud in sight. How could I tell him it simply doesn't rain this time of year? "Chase, it won't rain, honey. Look, no clouds; it's summer."

With PERFECT faith, he looked up at me and said, "Heavenly Father knows it's hot."

Two days later it rained.

As we grow older we seem to lose some of that trust and love for God. Earth life is a hard experience, and we bristle in all that trial.

All we need to start, though, to return to the right road on the journey, is just a little faith, a particle Alma said: "But behold, if ye will *awake* your faculties, even to an experiment upon my words, and *exercise a particle of faith,* yea, even if ye can no more than desire to believe, *let this desire work in you,* even until ye believe in a manner that ye can *give place* . . ." (Alma 32:27, emphasis added)

I heard it said once that habits are thick veils over our lives; we are creatures of habit. It takes hard work to change a negative habit! If you think "giving place" is a breeze, you may be mistaken.

To "give place" means to change—it will take change to use self-control, alter your thoughts, study diligently, and seek the best gifts.

Giving place requires change—perhaps a lot of changing . . .

Chapter  Three

Hope

"Where there is no hope, there can be no endeavor."
—*Samuel Johnson*

"How is it that ye can attain unto faith, save ye shall have hope? . . . Wherefore, if a man have faith, he must needs have hope." (Moroni 7:40, 42)

Have you ever hoped for something? Of course, you have. Someone once said that hope was the last thing that dies in man. When most people think of the word hope, however, they see it as a weak and wishful word. They use hope as an expression of a feeble wish that is overshadowed by strong doubt. (I hope it won't snow. I hope I won't get sick. I hope I marry a millionaire, etc.) So it makes us wonder why Moroni linked hope together with such mighty virtues as faith and charity. What does hope have to do with faith and charity?

What most people fail to realize is that a first definition of hope is not a wish but an EXPECTATION. In my dictionary (Webster's Collegiate) the synonym for hope is EXPECT. This sense of expectation, instead of wishing, makes all the difference in the world when the word hope appears in the scriptures! Read the following scriptures and substitute the word expect (or expectation) for hope:

"And again, my beloved brethren, I would speak unto you concerning hope. How is it that ye can attain unto faith, save ye shall have hope?" (Moroni 7:40)

"Be of good courage, and he shall strengthen your heart, all ye that hope in the Lord." (Psalms 31:24)

"Wherefore, whoso believeth in God might with surety hope for a better world, yea, even a place at the right hand of God, which hope cometh of faith, maketh an anchor to the souls of men, which would make them sure and steadfast, always abounding in good works, being led to glorify God." (Ether 12:4)

Hope, then, is an *expectation* of things to come. We must expect that we can become as Christ and inherit the Celestial Kingdom. You should expect, through faith and obedience, to be raised up to Eternal Life.

"And what is it that ye shall hope for? Behold I say unto you that ye shall have hope through the atonement of Christ and the power of his resurrection, to be raised unto life eternal, and this because of your faith in him according to the promise." (Moroni 7:41)

When I was a young girl, about twelve years old, I remember sitting in a sacrament meeting where the speaker kept apologizing for his talk. He kept saying that he didn't feel worthy to present the material. He felt others in the congregation were probably more qualified. He made it clear he didn't think he could inherit the Celestial Kingdom.

As the years passed, I heard that same attitude many times from members of the Church. I assumed that the Celestial Kingdom was going to be a place of only prophets. For a long time I believed that an ordinary woman like myself would probably never make it. It would require absolute perfection while here in mortality. It wasn't until I was in my middle twenties that I realized how contrary to the gospel of Jesus Christ that kind of thinking is!

The gospel actually helps us to have hope (expectations). The Lord wants us to hope. He says it's a requirement necessary for exaltation.

"And except ye have charity ye can in nowise be saved in the kingdom of God; neither can ye be saved in the kingdom of God if ye have not faith; *neither* can ye if ye have no *hope*." (Moroni 10:21, emphasis added)

Why, then, do significant numbers of us become discouraged with ourselves and lose hope in ourselves? What causes us to lose this hope so desperately needed?

I refer back to what I said in Chapter One:

1. We see the woman we really are and the one we can potentially become, the real versus the ideal. The two never really become one in mortal life, and sometimes the gap overwhelms us.

2. Our razor sharp consciousness of what others think of us causes us to cover up our inadequacies or frustrations by projecting only the positive. There is nothing wrong with that if we realize—*everyone else is doing the same thing!* But we forget that. Everyone else looks so "together" while we live daily with our imperfections.

3. Then there is Satan who discourages us by tempting, frustrating, or planting negative thinking in our minds.

4. We are trying as women to juggle so many roles and be the superwoman—supermormon. We are everything from taxi driver to laundress. If we aren't married with children, and all proper images, we feel guilty or cheated. We often seem to feel *fragmented*, never a Whole.

Instead of IDENTIFYING these negatives in ourselves and then trying to deal with them and exercise FAITH and HOPE, we try to remedy our discouragement by:

1. *Gossip or defame others*—it is so soul satisfying (we think at the moment) to pull others down to "our level." We criticize and find fault because we are threatened by the positive side of others. It relieves the tension for the moment—"Sister Jones just *can't* be *that* great. I stuck to her dirty kitchen floor this morning!" Or "Those are *the*

Sister Jones' kids hanging from the chandelier in the chapel!"

2. *We try to make others feel guilty* for *our* inadequacies. If we see a sister who seems to be different with her roles, we tactfully (?) let her know we disapprove: "You mean you *don't* can tomatoes?" "You've been married five years and *NO* children?" "You mean you *only* have three children?" "Why aren't *you* married?" and etc.

3. *We try to accumulate expensive signs* like cars, jewelry, house, furniture that say, "I am a success."

4. *We say, "I don't care"* about being a success.

Of course, none of these really work. I can say that because, except for number two, I have done or said all the others. I have been the recipient of number 2. They may soothe for the moment, but the effect wears off because they are superficial, and they are very wrong. It is behavior we must identify and STOP.

Our Savior suffered in Gethsemane and then on the cross at Calvary. He bled from every pore, He was mocked, teased, spat upon, whipped to near death, and then His flesh was gored and torn by driving nails through His hands and feet. Why?

He did it because He loved us—HE KNEW WE COULD MAKE IT AND BE LIKE HIM! Would He have put himself through that if He didn't EXPECT us to make it?

Don't you want to become what He KNOWS and EXPECTS you to be?

As you develop that knowledge in God and in the Savior, you will feel good about Them and love Them. That is faith. As you love Them and feel Their love for you, you will feel good about yourself and love yourself; you will expect more from yourself. That is Hope. And as you love yourself, you feel such a desire, not obligation, but a desire to love and serve others. That is charity. Hope is as mighty a virtue as faith and charity and does have a vital place with them!

Major Jay C. Hess, a pilot in the United States Air Force, was shot down August 24, 1967 fifteen miles south of the China border, northeast of Hanoi. He was captured by the North Vietnamese, and held as a prisoner of war five and one-half years. He was released March 14, 1973. At the time of his capture, Major Hess was 42 years old. Major Hess was from Bountiful, Utah, married and the father of five children. He was also a member of the Church of Jesus Christ of Latter-day Saints.

It was 3 p.m. August 24, 1967 as Major Hess (then Captain) was on his 31st mission. He had just dropped a bomb from the sleek F-15 aircraft he was piloting, when his plane was hit, and it immediately caught fire. Everything happened so fast—the last thing Captain Hess remembered was reaching for the ejection handle. The extreme speed and forces of flight rendered him unconscious as he floated from the flaming aircraft. His parachute just floated downward in the gaze of the waiting enemy soldiers. As he regained consciousness, he became aware of a lot of commotion. There were shots and shouts and overpowering Vietnamese.

At the direction of his captors, he walked for a couple of hours and reached a cave. Here he was given medical treatment for the wound on his neck and head. He was questioned about who he was and where he was from. He realized he was very much alone. As evening approached, Captain Hess was taken by jeep to various military units. Here he was shown off—and it was a very humilitating experience for him.

As night drew on Captain Hess was displayed at camp after camp—he had no rest. His mind was filled with baffling thoughts of what to do—what could he do? Finally, just before dawn, he was flown by helicopter to Hanoi. Here he was left alone naked in a prison.

It was nearly three weeks before he received the standard issue of clothing. He was hauled out of prison many times and interrogated. This was a period of much praying for him.

Captain Hess had read the *Doctrine and Covenants* just before he was shot down, as part of a project to study all the scriptures. The passages were fresh on his mind.

'When Joseph Smith was in prison, he offered some prayers for relief, and the answer the Lord gave him was that the ordeal would last for just a 'moment'.'

Brother Hess remembered the words of the scripture, 'My son, peace be unto thy soul; thine adversity and thine affliction shall be but a small moment.' (*Doctrine and Covenants* 121:7) From this scripture he gained strength as he offered his own prayers.

As he was alone for 40 days, he thought of the Savior's forty days in the wilderness. Many things came back to his mind—phrases and verses—'Don't give up, keep trying,' 'Press on,' 'Though the way be full of trials, weary not.' He remembered the stories of faith he had been taught since childhood. Brother Hess continually reflected on his values, his life. He thought of Farmington, Utah where he grew up, of all his friends there, and of his wife and family. He thought of the hymn book, and the songs he sang at church. Sundays were special for him and he decided to dedicate Sunday to the Lord for thought and prayer.

He thought it curious that the music of the Mormon Tabernacle Choir came to his mind so often—especially on Sunday mornings as he thought of his home and family. He didn't find out until four years later that his wife was singing with the choir.

Finally he had three roommates, and they often talked of their families and religion. He found out then and as time passed on that the prisoners he was associated with were impressed with the LDS family home evening program. 'Tell me the Mormon story again,' a roommate would say, and Brother Hess would tell the story of the Church and bear his testimony.

As the days passed by—Brother Hess thought, 'Eternity is forever. That is my anchor, eternal life!' He thought of his family often and prayed he could one day be with them again.

As his eyes scanned the dull, dingy plaster of his prison cell, he often thought, 'If only I had a Bible.' It had been such a long time since he had worked on his special project to read all the scriptures. It was against the rules for prisoners to talk to each other during those first years. Even with cell mates, conversation was secret, spoken in very low tones.

When after three years the prisoners were allowed to have a Bible for half a day on Saturday, the Vietnamese issued a pencil and paper so they could copy some scriptures. Brother Hess sat with the pencil in one hand and the Bible in the other—and thought, 'How I have missed a pencil.' As he copied the Sermon on the Mount—he also thought, 'I will write the parable of the Sower also, the first chapter of Genesis and the thirteenth chapter of First Corinthians, which deals with faith, hope, and charity, and some other scriptures that will be most valuable.' Brother Hess felt the strength of the scriptures. He could feel the courage of the Savior and the prophets.

Finally as the months passed, it appeared that there might be an opportunity to write a letter home. Brother Hess was very excited. He kept thinking, 'What can I write that will be of more value than anything else?' Then he decided, 'The thing I want most to tell my family is about eternal life.' He wrote the letter many times in his mind.

He knew exactly what he was going to say when at last he was escorted to a room, given a pencil and a piece of paper about 4×5 inches long and reminded to only write about health and family. This is what he wrote:

'Dearest Marjorie, Cameron, Heather, Warren, Holly, Heidi. Above all I seek for eternal life with all of you. These are important: temple marriage, mission, college. Press on. Set goals, write history, take pictures twice a year.'

These few words carried the message that brought new hope and tears of joy to his family in Bountiful, Utah.

The day Jay Hess left prison, he thought, 'How can I impress my family and children that eternal life is the most valuable possession? Then he decided, 'A pencil—when you live in a world where you have no means of writing, you learn to appreciate a pencil. If my children can appreciate being without means of writing things down, then maybe it will help them understand the significance of the loss of eternal life. I will put an 'EL' on the pencils to remind them of eternal life as they use the pencils.'

For three years Brother Hess' wife and family didn't know whether he was dead or alive. She said, 'Over the years I wondered. Why does it have to be so long? Anybody can endure something so long, but six years is such a long time to wait. During the entire time,' Mrs. Hess added, 'the strength that kept me going was the gospel. Sometimes the Lord teaches us that we have to wait for things in order for His works to go on as He knows best. While Jay was away, I developed and learned so much. The things I've learned have made me a better person. I feel it was for a purpose. It's helped me to understand things better. I have more empathy for people. I feel the Lord touched me with His finger, so to speak, and that I have been able to learn many great things. (*The Shadow of Death*, Chapters 15, 16, 17)

Major Hess and His wife demonstrated great faith and hope. In developing those qualities they learned compassion and empathy for others and charity. These three are not only interrelated, they are interdependent!

If we are to develop hope and learn to expect great things from ourselves and our future, there are specifics that we *must* do:

1. Have priorities
2. Have goals
3. Be creative
4. Have patience

Have Priorities

A priority is some act or element that needs a place of importance or immediate attention. When there is not a definite outline for priorities, or if we have not come to grips with our priorities, there is absolutely no chance of gaining hope. *When priorities (and that feeling of peace that what you are doing at that moment is important) are missing, you find yourself floundering in complete frustration.* It's called "feeling fragmented." That kind of frustration kills hope and self-expectation, and you can hardly get past the laundry.

What is it that we need in order to adjust *and feel good* about our priorities? The first thing we need is a proper understanding about TIME.

Neal Maxwell said, "God does not begin by asking about our *ability* but only about our *availability* and if we then prove our *dependability,* he will increase our *capability.*" (Emphasis added)

My father is the director of the name extraction program in his stake. It requires a minimum of twelve hours' service each week from the members who serve as extractors. They are on their own as to time given; no one stands over them with a whip. They are dedicated servants of God, and my father has grown to love them deeply.

What Neal Maxwell said is evident in every dedicated name extractor. They were called, not because of their ability, (in fact, none had any ability) but because of their availability. In other words, they were *willing* to be available to work for the Lord. Those who have shown their dedication and dependability have grown, no, blossomed in their capability.

There was one young man, however, who saddened my father. He was called, and he accepted. He came out regularly for a few weeks, then his hours began to dwindle, and soon he wasn't coming at all. He came to my dad and asked to be released. He said he was playing on a baseball team, and genealogy interferred with his games.

Instead of trying to work out a schedule around the games or following through with his commitment—even if it meant no baseball for that year—he asked to be released.

My father was hurt for this young man. He asked me, "What do you think is the most expensive time on television, Anita?" I didn't know. He said, "The television program 60 Minutes is the most expensive time there is. It costs advertisers about $150,000 per minute to advertise on that show. It is the *prime time* of the nation."

He went on, "That's what the Lord is asking from us, Anita, *prime time,* the most expensive time we have. It's not the same thing if we give Him leftover time or time at our convenience. He will bless us in our abilities if we will give Him prime time!"

Being the women we are today, there are so many roles to juggle, and somewhere in the middle of it we want to come out with something for ourselves. Understanding that there is a time for everything is the place to start.

As we understand Time, it is so important to remember it falls into three categories:

1. The DAILY living—our present day-to-day tasks.
2. The MONTHLY responsibilities.
3. The LIFETIME or OVERALL responsibilities.

Prime Time, however, belongs to the Lord.

As the Women of God, we should be giving strict attention to what we are doing during our Prime Time. Our priorities should be in this order:

1. Seek first the kingdom of God with all our heart (emotion and feeling), might (self-discipline), mind (intellect and thought), and strength (time and energy).
2. Have goals: daily, lifetime, and eternal goals.
3. Seek the companionship and direction of the Holy Ghost by praying for it and living worthy to receive it.
4. Take care of our physical bodies by proper diet and exercise so that we can feel good and physically be prepared to handle our responsibilities.
5. Love, honor, and respect our husbands. We must work hard to be *companions* to them.
6. Be a righteous Mother in Zion.
7. Strengthen our extended families, parents, brothers, and sisters, and etc. Love them, elevate them, and add our testimonies to their lives.
8. Magnify our church callings and be willing to serve the Lord.
9. Serve our fellowman in any way we possibly can.
10. Develop our talents and intellectual capacity in order to serve the Lord more and increase our potential.

It is vital to remember that these priorities are all interrelated and have to be worked on at the same time! That's where the discouragement comes. But you can change all that if you will look at those priorities in the realm of DAILY, MONTHLY, and LIFETIME. Let's look at each priority in that manner:

Daily

1. Seek the Kingdom of God—
   Read the scriptures each day.
   Pray morning and evening.
2. Set goals—
   Write down each morning what you need to accomplish for the day in order of importance; cross them off as you finish. If you don't finish, add them to the next day.
3. Seek the spirit—
   You've already asked for it in your prayer, now take time throughout the day to *pay attention* to the spirit.
4. Take care of your physical body—
   Exercise, even ten minutes each day.
   Eat properly.
5. Love your husband—
   If you will do something each day to serve your husband, you will find your love for him strengthen. Say, "I love you" each day.
6. Be a righteous mother—
   Try to inspire your children each day. Love them.
   Attend to their immediate needs; have family prayer daily. If possible be home. As a homemaker, you should teach children order by keeping your home and yards clean. Have them do a chore each day.
7. Strengthen your family—
   On a daily basis, include them in your prayers.

8. Magnify Church callings—

    Take a few minutes each day to *ponder* what you can do to improve your effort. Pray over your stewardships.

9. Serve others—

    Be ready to help; pay attention to opportunities that may come your way.

10. Develop your potential—

    Find time each day, even if only ten minutes, to refuel and fill your spirit. Read a good book, talk to a friend, buy a new dress, work on a hobby.

Monthly

1. Seek the Kingdom of God—

    If you have been to the temple, attend it regularly.

    Attend all your meetings.

    Keep the Sabbath Day holy.

    Keep the commandments.

2. Set goals—

    The first of every month *write down* what you need to accomplish for the month in order of importance.

3. Seek the spirit—

    Fast on Fast Sunday.

4. Take care of your physical body—

    Lose weight if necessary; exercise and eat properly.

5. Love your husband—

    Concentrate on building and developing this relationship.

    Go on dates; have projects together.

6. Be a righteous mother—

    Have family home evening each week.

    Support them in their school and church work.

    Teach them gospel principles in every moment or example possible.

7. Strengthen your family—
   Write letters or visit them.
   Hold family get-togethers.
   Express your love.
8. Magnify Church callings—
   Attend all your auxiliary meetings.
   Do your visiting teaching.
   Study.
   Be dependable.
9. Serve others—
   Minister to the sick and needy.
   Be a missionary.
10. Develop your potential—
    Take a class or begin a new hobby or continue to be educated in your specific areas of interest by reading and practicing.

Lifetime

1. Seek the Kingdom of God—
   Stick to your commitments and covenants.
   Obey the Prophet (acquire food storage, plant a garden, keep a journal, do genealogy, etc.).
2. Set goals—
   Each January *write down* your goals for the year and for your life — reevaluate year to year.
3. Seek the spirit—
   Obey the spirit and try to be teachable so that you can continue growing.
4. Take care of your physical body—
   Have regular yearly check-ups.
5. Love your husbands—
   Demonstrate in word and deed your love.

6. Be a righteous mother—
    You are a mother forever. Teach your children by word and deed that your support and love is eternal.
    Set an example.
    Leave something of value (spiritually) for your posterity.
7. Strengthen your family—
    Do genealogy.
    Support them in all their righteous endeavors (attend reunions, missionary farewells, blessings, etc., where possible).
8. Magnify Church callings—
    Never feel you have done enough. You should accept callings until you die.
9. Serve others—
    Continue to be a missionary.
    If possible, increase your fast offerings and support the missionary fund.
10. Develop your potential—
    Spend time to further your world around you.
    Travel, take classes, be curious, read.
    Take time for yourself.

These are just overall views of how it is possible to accomplish many things when we look at priorities in short-range and long-range views. When establishing your priorities, you should use this list as a guideline only, and adapt it to the specific needs of yourself, your family and your circumstances.

The secret, however, in making a list of priorites *really work* is to be FLEXIBLE! Now I don't mean so flexible that before long the list has no resemblance to its original, and you are right back where you were, running ragged, accomplishing nothing, and losing hope.

You should have some definite *non-negotiable* lifetime, monthly, and daily priorities that cannot be ignored or abandoned. Being flexible means that you will be able to shift or adjust the *negotiable* priorities in order to meet the demands of the non-negotiable ones. For example, if you have planned to clean your kitchen cupboards for the day (negotiable priority—it can be placed in another time slot) and your child (non-negotiable priority—motherhood is forever) comes to you with a need to talk or be loved for a few hours, the cupboards can wait, and you should not feel frustrated. At a moment like this, think of the cupboards in terms of flexibility and motherhood as a fixed priority.

There will be those occasions from time to time, however, that will make it necessary for you to place TOP priority to a certain commitment on a temporary basis. If you are the roadshow director, it may mean that on performance nights your family won't see you for several days. If the farmer's cow is in the ditch, he cannot leave him there to die. No matter the day of the week, or hour of the day, he is responsible to his commitment as owner of the cow to pull him out.

I personally am learning the value of priorities by trial and error. But there are some definites in my list of priorities that are non-negotiable. And I have freedom from frustration of how I *feel* about them. These are seeking the kingdom and being a good wife and mother. Even though all the other priorities are inter-related, these are foremost in my heart, and I truly concentrate most efforts there.

The first year after my graduation I freelanced and was "at home" with my baby son. The second year I worked out of necessity. But I couldn't help feeling guilty because I was enjoying working. It was a terrible experience to leave my child every-day, having him sob in my arms and then be in turmoil all day because of my guilt for leaving him and yet enjoying my job. The added digs and stabs from well-meaning (and some not so well-meaning) relatives caused me to suffer until I could no longer stand it. That's when I went in to the Lord and came back with a most *personal* message that "these were things I came with!"

But the other part of that message was my responsibility as wife and mother—motherhood being a partnership with God. And so I began my life of trial and error with priorities.

I made covenants that my family would always come first and promised them I would always be there when they needed me. It has been a terrific price to pay at times, and sometimes I have had to manage on very little sleep. It has taken every ounce of strength I have had to schedule priorities so that I could be a *full-time* wife and mother.

A few years ago someone commented to me (upon learning that I have always left work in time to be there when the children get home from school), "Boy! You have it made, working such easy hours!" I just looked at him with a blank stare; not one of my hours has been easy. Anyone who has worked with me can describe how much I push myself; manufacturers' reps know they can't "drop" in because every minute is accounted for. There are no casual lunches and no social visits. All is at this pace for one reason—to get home in time to attend to the needs of my family—little league, dance lessons, piano, speech therapy, family home evening, dinner, laundry, stories, and being together.

Everything has been working great until this past year. Whereas in the past I have been able to establish priorities and go with the flow, now suddenly things have changed. I was able to take my children to work with me since they were infants. I was able to juggle my schedules to meet theirs. Our store has been reflective of the activities of children—mirrors smeared with little handprints, toys tucked in carpet samples, half eaten animal crackers on table tops, and baby bottles in the refrigerator.

But now I find that my children are no longer little ones around my feet who are content to have their bottom dry, nose wiped, and a new story read to them or game played. Now I am the mother of a teenager and pre-teen who are demanding adult attention and conversation. They have near-adult problems and challenges ahead. I also have a five-year-old who is "going on 21," and we recently adopted a baby. Suddenly my family has changed. I find myself stretched from adult attention of teenagers to the totally consuming tasks of a helpless infant.

And then another dimension has been added: I am trying to stand up and be counted for the Lord's rights for women.

All of this has added up to one decision; it is time to reshuffle priorities. The non-negotiable ones can't be moved, so I must start where it is most obvious. It is no longer possible for me to be "fully present" at home when I am under such demands externally in the business. Therefore, I need to "cut back" on my business activities and "semi-retire."

If someone said two years ago that this is where my thoughts would be today, I would have laughed! I was in complete control then. Today, too much has changed. There is no going back. I can only move forward and onward to the next changes.

Priorities need to be flexible and constantly reevaluated. When the time comes to alter them, no matter the personal sacrifice, priorities need to be changed.

Priorities also need to be on individual terms. As Mormon women we have been taught what womanhood and motherhood is. We know, *eternally* know what it is, because we feel familiar with all the aspects of womanhood. But we damage our self-esteem and cause others to suffer when we try to structure ourselves and every woman according to how *we* perceive the priority list should be. Let me illustrate:

In the heart of most women is a desire and need to be at home. Lately I have seen so many articles on the "Working Mom versus Non-Working Mom." It seems there is a who-can-make-who-feel-the-guiltiest-movement going on! I have even received letters from women who want to stay home but are beginning to fell guilty!

Those who choose to work are met with a legion of people reminding them of the children they are neglecting. Those who choose to stay home are met by an opposite legion reminding them of their lack of ambition or brains. I ask you, whose right is it to destroy another's free agency? Whose right is it to question another's thoughtful and prayerful decision?

Now some of you may say, "How do you know their decision was prayerful?" We don't. It's really none of our business. It is not our duty to stand up and criticize another person for any of their choices. What is our duty?

1. Follow the Prophet. Listen to his council. Be very, very careful about our own decisions, whatever they are in regard to. Make sure our choices are prayerful and meet with the Lord's approval.

2. Clearly understand what the Lord requires and expects of us as wives, mothers, women, sisters. *Our priorities should be on His terms.* The role of women whether married or single is an exact partnership with the priesthood. We should be anxiously engaged in teaching our young women the blessings of being a woman, the necessity to expand her mind, and the value of "working in the home."

3. Each woman should be establishing her *own* priorities, based on her *own* circumstances.

I have spent a lot of words on Working Mothers. It's been a way for me to relate to time and priorities. But it is also such a controversial issue because more and more women in the Church are going to work. As the economic conditions worsen, and they are going to, more of you will become working mothers out of necessity. Many more of you may have to work because you divorce or because your husband dies or becomes disabled. You need never feel the anguish of guilt if you will use your priorities with utmost care. Both you and your family will be blessed for your careful efforts, and you will feel great strength from the Lord.

The world is screaming at women that they are unfulfilled and "a homebody nobody" if they aren't seeking a career. It's just a Satanic plot to destroy the home labeled "Women's Rights." The Lord has rights for women, too! These are rights you were born with:

The right to be Unique.
The right to Motherhood.
The right to be a member of the Church.
The right to share the Priesthood.
The right to be Respected.

Each woman should be establishing her *own* priorities, based on her *own* circumstances. This is a great letter I received from a mother of four:

> I am a mother of four (ages 1-5), and this last year has seen great changes: a barage of work with three church callings, feelings of depression, low self-esteem, anger, confusion, a loss of the spirit. I had never seen such dark hours. I yelled at and spanked my kids; I withdrew from my husband. I didn't understand why I felt certain feelings, why my house always was so unkept, the diaper pail overflowing. Why wasn't I as organized, as pretty, as skinny as a mother of eight in my ward? What was wrong with me?

This woman went on to tell me of a gift of some motivational tapes she received. Then she attended an education week and read some pertinent books on self-esteem. She began to IDENTIFY what was wrong. It started with her priorities. She was trying to compete with the "Mormon Mold Image." She was trying to compete with everyone except herself. She had no daily, monthly, lifetime priorities. She went on:

> I found I am not competing with Camilla Kimball for Heavenly Father's love. I am loved just for me and just for *my efforts*. I don't have to go crazy because of so much responsibility. I can be responsible to put priorities back into my life. I don't need THREE church callings. My higher calling is teaching our children about love and family and choices. No one can reach our children like us women.
>
> I have relearned the value of priorities. I have started trying harder to compete with only me, then be a wife, then a mother. This last year I have gone from crying daily to recently finishing three of four Easter dresses for a sister who has cancer and can't sew for her girls. I feel a

joy in service. I feel a feeling of "thank you" from Heavenly Father. I have turned around. I am supporting my husband. I'm loving our children. I'm working on growing closer to our Heavenly Parents. I am establishing priorities!

Can you see how she really has identified and taken control of her *Prime Time?* She has her priorities carefully evaluated and is maintaining flexibility.

It is obvious from my books that I believe a woman *should* and *must* continue to progress academically and intellectually as well as spiritually. You can do that no matter what your role in life is or *where* you find yourself.

I have heard it said by some in the Church that you must put *everything* aside and just be a mother. Then when your children are grown, you can have something for yourself. Again, I say, ridiculous! HOW CAN YOU GIVE A DRINK FROM AN EMPTY WELL?

If you are using your priorities properly, you can have something, even a little something, for yourself right NOW. It will take evaluation of your daily, monthly, and lifetime routines and goals. It will take prayer and inspiration from the Holy Ghost. It will take flexibility. And it will take *a lot* of common sense!

"Do not run faster or labor more than you have strength and means." *(Doctrine and Covenants* 10:4)

I watched my little daughter walk on the beach one summer and collect every shell in sight. When the day came to go home, she couldn't take the entire collection; there would have been no room for suitcases. She had to be selective and take only the most beautiful ones. Today they are still her prizes.

You can't collect all the shells on the beach. You can't do *everything.* Be selective. Make the most of your days and months and years. Pack many moments with quality and action and have some that soothe the soul, too.

Set Goals

The mighty apostle Paul had the chance to appear before King Agrippa and discuss the charges that were against him. King Agrippa wanted to hear Paul speak. He was really intrigued

As Paul spoke, he did so with the spirit of the Holy Ghost. He began to tell the King of his encounter on Damascus road with Jesus Christ, the Savior of the world. His words rang with power and authority:

> At midday, O King, I saw in the way a light from heaven, above the brightness of the sun, shining round about me and them which journeyed with me.
>
> And when we were all fallen to the earth, I heard a voice speaking unto me, and saying in the Hebrew tongue, Saul, Saul, why persecutest thou me? It is hard for thee to kick against the pricks.
>
> And I said, Who art thou, Lord? And he said, I am Jesus whom thou persecutest.
>
> But rise, and stand upon thy feet: for I have appeared unto thee for this purpose, to make thee a minister and a witness both of these things which thou hast seen, and of those things in the which I will appear unto thee;
>
> Delivering thee from the people, and from the Gentiles, unto whom now I send thee,
>
> To open their eyes, and to turn them from darkness to light, and from the power of Satan unto God that they may receive forgiveness of sins, and inheritance among them which are sanctified by faith that is in me. (Acts 26: 13-18)

Paul then told him that he was obedient and had been going about the country calling the people to repentance. He bore his testimony that he knew the work was true and that Jesus was the son of God who suffered and died to be resurrected. He bore a fervent witness and said he spoke the truth, and he stated that he knew King Agrippa believed. He then addressed the King:

> King Agrippa, believest thou the prophets? I know that thou believest.
>
> Then Agrippa said unto Paul, *Almost* thou persuadest me to be a Christian. (Acts 26:27-28, emphasis added)

So close did King Agrippa come to accepting the gospel and being saved. So close did he come to a chance for exaltation. *Almost* he said.

Almost sounds like you nearly reached your goal. It "almost" sounds noteworthy. But in truth it is so far away. "I almost learned to sew" sounds close, but what have you made that you can wear to show you *almost* learned? "I almost learned how to plant a garden." (Where is the garden?) "I almost quit smoking" (as you light another cigarette). "I almost repented" (as the sin is repeated).

Almost implies you were very close to the goal. What happened to cause you to topple back? What about the small percent it would have taken if you were that close? You cannot "almost" pay tithes, do visiting teaching, attend church, etc. You either do it, or you don't.

I am amazed at how many people go through life without any goals. They live day to day, accepting whatever comes their way. They go from day to day and year to year just existing and letting whatever "falls" in their lap be their life. They have no goals, no strategy, and in that sense, no future! You should look at the priorities list and be able to have goals in each category.

To establish and achieve goals you must:

1. "SEEK YE FIRST THE KINGDOM OF GOD" (Matthew 6:33)
   Make sure your goal is a righteous one. Would the Lord approve? If your intentions are pure, you will have inspiration in selecting proper goals in your life. Always refer to your priorities list when selecting worthy goals.

2. BE SPECIFIC
   Set clearly in your mind EXACTLY what it is you want to accomplish and HOW you are going to do it. Your goal must be specific, and you must picture how you are going to accomplish it. A good way to plan is by asking yourself:
   What am I going to do?
   When am I going to do it?

How am I going to do it?
Who could help me?
Where can I do it?
How long do I need?
Why am I going to do this?

3. WRITE IT DOWN

There is a real strength in writing down goals. When you ponder goals, ideas come to you. As quickly as one comes, it can leave you or become confused as other thoughts appear. Writing down goals and ideas help secure the thought process. They become more permanent. Keep a separate notebook or journal, even just for goals and ideas. Refer to it often. If necessary, repeat your goal aloud during the day.

I have a friend who has written down the goal for her eternal life. A little piece of paper taped inside a kitchen cupboard door says, "I am going home." She repeats that aloud at breakfast, lunch, and dinner. She'll make it to the Celestial Kingdom; it is her goal. Keeping it constantly forward in her daily thoughts helps her live more earnestly each day.

President Kimball said, "We must have goals to make progress, encouraged by keeping records . . . progress is easier when it is timed, checked, and measured. Goals are good. Laboring with distant aim sets the mind in a higher key and puts us at our best. Goals should always be made to a point that will make us reach and strain."

4. REPORT YOUR GOALS

Go to that journal and notebook and record your progress. You should also include the Lord (even a friend, spouse, or child) in your goals. You should ask the Lord for His approval and also report your progress.

Thomas S. Monson said, "When performance is measured, performance improves. When performance is measured and reported, performance accelerates."

Tell Him of your desires and commitments. Don't you think He is interested? Would you be interested in hearing your child's goals?

Reporting goals outloud is motivating because it makes the goal more of a *sure* commitment. We are also motivated to "save face." But the main objective in discussing goals aloud is that it checks our progress. It keeps the clutter off the road and helps us clearly to see how far we've come.

5. SET REALISTIC GOALS

There are short-range goals and long-range goals. They tie in with your DAILY, MONTHLY, and LIFETIME priorities. A short-range goal would be: take piano lessons and practice one hour a day. A long-range goal would be: give a recital and teach others.

Remember, *Competence Creates Confidence.* Having a few repeated successes will help you gain confidence in tackling more difficult ones. All goals should make us reach; some should make us strain. Don't set goals, however, that are improbable. If I set a goal to be an Olympic swimmer right now, it is highly improbable for me to make it. My age, for one thing, but my other priorities wouldn't allow the time necessary. If you set an improbable goal, or improbable time limit, and you don't meet that goal, your confidence will weaken, and you will have not benefitted from that goal. Start with simple ones and then add the more difficult ones.

6. COMMIT TO THEM

President Kimball's now famous motto declares "Do It!" What good is any plan, no matter how strong the desire to succeed, if ACTION doesn't take place.

I once hired a floral designer because she marched into my office and presented her goals to me with an enthusiasm that left me sparkling. She told me what she could do for my company and why. She listed her goals for herself and our firm. I was so impressed! Within one week I knew it was all "go and no-show." Talk is cheap. (In the design business we are supposed to say "inexpensive!") That enthusiasm was there, and she talked and talked. But I didn't see any action. I gave her the benefit of the doubt. At the end of four weeks, the enthusiasm had paled, nothing was accomplished, and she was dismissed. Goals without action equal nothing.

"Help us, oh God, to remember that little things completed are better than big things planned." (Peter Marshall)

7. THE NEXT LEVEL

A goal should be the next level and not the final result! Most people become frustrated when they plan for a goal, then upon reaching it, they level off. If temple marriage is your goal, and you reach it, then other goals need to be established quickly to make the marriage a success. Always plan your goals with the next level in mind.

Be Creative

How can you possibly have *hope* in your abilities and talents if you are not effectively using and developing them?

"My feeling is that each of us has the potential for special accomplishment in some field. The opportunities for women to excel are greater today than ever before. We should all be resourceful and ambitious, expanding our interests." (Camilla Kimball, *Blueprints for Living*, Volume 1, page 23)

The Savior walked and talked with sinners. He had association with liars, thieves, murderers, harlots, publicans, adulterers, and the self-righteous. He was benevolent to them all, even in parable. Except on one occasion. In one parable He was almost merciless to the sinner. It was the parable of the ten talents:

> Then he which had received the one talent came and said, Lord, I knew thee that thou art an hard man, reaping where thou hast not sown, and gathering where thou hast not strawed:
>
> And I was afraid, and went and hid thy talent in the earth: lo, there thou hast that is thine.
>
> His lord answered and said unto him, Thou wicked and slothful servant, thou knewest that I reap where I sowed not, and gather where I have not strawed:
>
> Thou oughtest therefore to have put my money to the exchangers, and then at my coming I should have received mine own with usury.
>
> Take therefore the talent from him, and give it unto him which hath ten talents.
>
> For unto every one that hath shall be given, and he shall have abundance: but from him that hath not shall be taken away even that which he hath.
>
> And cast ye the unprofitable servant unto outer darkness: there shall be weeping and gnashing of teeth.
> (Matthew 25:24-30)

The master had given the servant one talent, and the servant went out and buried it. When confronted with his stewardship, the servant offered a grumbling excuse that he thought the Lord didn't sow where he had reaped. He was trying to bring the Lord down to his level. The Lord replied that since he believed this, all the more reason the servant should have used his talent more wisely. In verse 27, the Lord says that he should have at least put it in the bank so He could have gotten interest on it! In verse 29, the Lord gives a commandment "for unto every one that hath shall be given, and he shall have abundance: but from him that hath not shall be taken away even that which he hath."

Everyone is given at least some talent. And it is a commandment to use them so that the Lord can give us more. But if we don't use what we have, even that will be taken away.

> Every [woman] must use such talents as [she] may have or they will be lost. If a [woman] cannot compose music, perhaps [she] can sing in the choir; if [she] cannot

write books, at least [she] can read them; if [she] cannot
paint pictures, [she] can learn to appreciate the artistry
of others; if [she] cannot achieve preeminence in one
specific field, so be it, [she] still can succeed in [her] own
field; for each [woman] has some talent, and [she] will be
judged on the basis of how [she] uses what [she] has.

It is an eternal law of life that [we] either progress
or retrogress; [we] either increase [our] talents and
abilities, or those [we] have wither and die. No one stands
still; there is no such thing as pure neutrality. (*New
Testament Commentary*, McConkie, page 689)

In verse 30, the Lord casts the servant into outer darkness.
That almost seems merciless. Elder McConkie comments on
"Outer Darkness" with one word, "HELL." (*New Testament
Commentary*, McConkie, page 689) I think the Lord used outer
darkness to make two points. Our creativity is *that* important to
Him. It seriously offends Him if we throw away our gifts. Why?
Because the essence of Godhood is Creativity!

Even we are the product of creation.

The second point is that if we do lose our talents and they are
taken away and given to someone else, it would be like being in
hell. Someone once wrote: "Of all the words of tongue and pen,
saddest are these, 'what might have been.'"

In being creative you again have to make reference to and use
of your priorities and goals. You have to be selective and
discriminating in where you place your efforts. I have seen the
"jack-of-all-relief-society projects" and "master-of-none" so often
around me. I have heard women frustrated because they feel they
have no talents and are consumed by boxes of unfinished
projects. It is because they are back on that treadmill of
competing with everyone around them and not looking to their
own uniqueness.

You can be *guaranteed* you have been given at least one talent
or gift. ". . . to every man is given a gift. . ." (*Doctrine and
Covenants* 46:11)

It may not be in the area you want it to be, but you have at least *one* talent. I always wanted to be a great singer. Maybe even another Barbra Streisand. I could almost picture myself at Carnegie Hall belting it out! Once my brothers caught me in front of a mirror going through all the arm and hand motions of a singing star. I had to hide from them in public for months!

It was my clarinet teacher who said it tactfully to my mother. He wanted her to know I had absolutely no musical ability or singing voice. He said, "Anita has a good ear, she just isn't able to reproduce the sounds she hears." (Ah, well—maybe in the next life.)

I have a friend who spent a small fortune and about ten years trying to learn how to oil paint. She has absolutely no talent for it. One day she asked me what I thought—honestly. Tactfully I told her that her ceramics and sculptures were quality and truly art, and that's where her talent was. She agreed! She said she had been struggling to paint because she felt all artists should be able to paint. She didn't even like it.

Over the past two years she has concentrated her time on her sculpture and ceramics, and her last piece sold for $750! She had a *familiar feeling* for that art media and always knew it.

Talents are not only in the arts, like music, painting, drama, sculpture, and dance. They are in spiritual and social gifts as well.

A few Spiritual gifts are:

> Faith
> Humility
> Testimony
> Discernment
> Interpretation

A few Social gifts are:

> Cheerfulness
> Ability to put people at ease
> Teacher
> Listener, counselor
> Leadership

How do you discover where your talents lie? It's easy. *Pay attention.*

Is there something you do or say that causes others to compliment you often? Do you notice those same compliments over and over? (I love your smile; you do such a good job teaching the five-year-olds; your hair always looks so nice; etc.) Is there something that you say or do that seems to come easy to you, such as giving a talk, baking bread, sewing, etc? Is there something you say or do that, although you don't actively pursue it, seems familiar to you, such as poetry, painting, fixing up your home, counseling others?

You discover your talents by paying attention. Age has nothing to do with it; any age can produce a new talent.

A woman once told me she thought she had no talents. It shocked me. She was a good artist and had mastered calligraphy in addition to many homemaking skills. She did not consider these talents because she had never given them thought in that scope. They had become second nature, and she had only done them for her own entertainment.

I had the same experience. I just did tasks as they came along; it was part of me. I never really considered them talents, just part of my industrious life and work. As others began to point out my talents, I had to stop and think, "Yes, these are special gifts." Once recognized as such, I was better able to concentrate efforts to develop them and even recognize other ones.

Your talents have been given to you for wise purposes known by the Lord. "To some is given one, and to some is given another, that all may be profited thereby." (*Doctrine and Covenants* 46:12)

In order for you to profit by these and also for others to profit from your talents, you must be earnestly seeking to *find* them and *develop* them.

There is a little fairy tale about a boy who captures a star with a kite. The star's name is Acabar, and he teaches the boy that heavenly secrets are to be found right here on earth. Here is what he says about talents:

Along with the power of choice you received the most precious gift our Creator can bestow: The spark of life. With it came an obligation to apply your own special talents, whatever they may be, to leave this world a better place than you found it. Billions of humans have failed in this obligation and wasted their lives. (Og Mandino, *The Gift of Acabar,* page 58)

Let's add one more thing: To leave this earth a *better person* than when you came.

It doesn't matter if you have only ONE, and it seems as if others have multiple talents. Study, learn, practice, and develop that talent until you become proficient, confident, and master of it. An amazing process will begin to unfold. The mastery of one talent opens doors to others.

This is a true story of how a talent can develop:

A woman I know:

> Liked to hear poetry. (It was comfortable to her ear, seemed familiar.)
>
> Enjoyed reading it.
>
> Read it aloud to others.
>
> Seemed to develop a style of reading it that others enjoyed; she was asked to read it often.
>
> Found herself thinking poetic thoughts.
>
> Used poetic phrases.
>
> Began to express her feelings in poetic style.
>
> Began to write poetry.
>
> Took classes and studied poetry.
>
> Wrote more fluent poetry (and now prose).
>
> Her poetry was enjoyed by others.
>
> She taught a class.
>
> She began to write lyrics for music.
>
> She was asked to sing her lyrics.
>
> She was asked to sing with other groups.
>
> She found a love and enjoyment in singing. (It was familiar to her.)
>
> Through lessons and practice, she developed that singing

ability and received recognition for it.

She was asked to write poems and songs for special events and programs; she tried to print with the pen in an attractive style.

She began to practice calligraphy.

She took lessons in calligraphy.

Soon she was being asked to hand-letter posters, programs, and special measages.

As she became familiar with a drawing tool, she experimented with sketching.

She found a "knack" for sketching and drawing.

She took lessons and practiced, and soon she was really drawing.

This woman who thought she had NO talent has developed an ability to write poetry and prose, sing, do calligraphy, and draw. This is because she paid attention to what felt familiar to her. She was simply re-learning what she already knew.

When we are familiar or comfortable with something, like enjoying poetry, we think everyone else is too. We don't realize that what is kindred to one is not to another. My husband is musically talented. I am not. I enjoy listening to good music, but I do not "hear" or "sense" the different instruments or rhythms like he does. He will make a comment about a song that has totally passed me. When you begin to pay attention to your familiarity with a talent or gift, or interest, you will be closer to knowing your true talents.

How you develop your talents is again combined with priorities and goals. Finding and applying the time is done in balance with your other responsibilities. In developing your talents, *it is not* so important that you be better than anyone else—the important thing is that you just make a contribution. I heard a 93-year-old lady who lived in a rest home say, "You have to give something back to life. The worst thing isn't growing old or even dying. The worst thing is dying while you are still alive!" She was vivacious, vibrant, and very creative. She was responsible for organizing a health club, a soccer club, a tennis club, and etc., within her rest home. If patients couldn't go to the activities, she created ingenious ways for the activities to come to them. She was making a contribution.

Probably one of the most inspiring stories of creativity comes from the *Book of Mormon* and the Brother of Jared.

Having built the barges as he had been commanded, he went to the Lord with two problems: how to get fresh air and how to light them. The Lord gave him instructions on the matter of the air, probably because it was out of the experience of their world at that time. But as to the matter of light, this was something the Brother of Jared could relate to. The Lord gave him no solution. A second time he went to the Lord with the question. This time the Lord questioned him in return, "What will ye that I should do that ye may have light in your vessels?" Then the Brother of Jared realized it was up to him to figure out what to do.

In faith, with careful, *creative thought,* he cut out sixteen small transparent stones. He carried them up a mountain where he sought out the Lord and asked Him to touch each of the stones with His finger that they might give light. It is a most tender account of how the Lord touched each one, and the Brother of Jared was able to see Him.

> And behold, O Lord, in them there is no light; whither shall we steer? And also we shall perish, for in them we cannot breathe, save it is the air which is in them; therefore we shall perish.
>
> And the Lord said unto the brother of Jared: Behold, thou shalt make a hole in the top, and also in the bottom; and when thou shalt suffer for air thou shalt unstop the hole and receive air. And if it be so that the water come in upon thee, behold, ye shall stop the hole, that ye may not perish in the flood.
>
> . . . Therefore what will ye that I should prepare for you that ye may have light when ye are swallowed up in the depths of the sea?
>
> And it came to pass that the brother of Jared went forth unto the mount, and did molten out of a rock

sixteen small stones; and they were white and clear, even as transparent glass; and he did carry them in his hands upon the top of the mount, and cried again unto the Lord, saying:

. . . behold these things which I have molten out of the rock.

And I know, O Lord, that thou hast all power, and can do whatsoever thou wilt for the benefit of man; therefore touch these stones, O Lord, with thy finger, and prepare them that they may shine forth in darkness; and they shall shine forth unto us in the vessels which we have prepared, that we may have light while we shall cross the sea.

Behold, O Lord, thou canst do this. We know that thou art able to show forth great power, which looks small unto the understanding of men.

And it came to pass that when the brother of Jared had said these words, behold, the Lord stretched forth his hand and touched the stones one by one with his finger. And the veil was taken from off the eyes of the brother of Jared, and he saw the finger of the Lord; and it was as the finger of a man, like unto flesh and blood; and the brother of Jared fell down before the Lord . . . (Ether 2:19-25, 3:1-6)

The Lord *expects* us to use our creativity. But in doing so, we must understand that we belong to the Lord. He bought us with His blood. We need to show gratitude for our *GIFTS* by taking care of them and using them with pure hearts and pure intentions. Use them to serve the Lord and not ourselves. This sister discovered that exact message:

It has been almost a year ago when the feeling first struck me. After having two kids and a daycare, I felt my days just couldn't fit anything else in, yet still I longed for something more. It was then I noticed my old guitar, dusty, waiting in the corner of our family room. I picked it up and tried a few chords. I could tell it had been too long. I decided maybe I needed to practice more . . . So I did.

Each afternoon after I got the kids down I would play

and sing, and pretty soon I felt I wanted to do more. Encouraged by my husband, I sought to find an outlet for my enjoyment of singing. Just singing to the four walls of my home didn't give me much enthusiasm for it.

Next my efforts turned to perhaps doing programs and earning money. Yes, that was it, that must be why I feel so compelled, so drawn to do something I decided.

That night I went to the temple to see my sister receive her endowments, but all during the first hour my mind and heart were troubled. 'Why am I so confused; I feel pulled into using my talent more, and yet I can find real peace since I first picked up my guitar two months ago. Why, all I want to do is perform and really use what I've got.' The battle in my mind would not let me concentrate on what was going on. It was really a fight.

Then after making a promise and covenant, I felt as though a 1,000 ton weight were lifted off my shoulders, and I sat down again; I knew my answer, 'With an eye single to the glory of God.'

Yes, that truly spoke peace to my troubled soul. I knew if I always used my talent for God and His purposes I would be given the strength to develop more talent and do all the many other things I'm called upon to do.

I came home and two days later accepted an invitation to do an Easter program for the Deseret Industries. The program was so simple for me to work out and the order so fun. Although I'd never really done much in this way before it seemed simple, yet the others in the quartet I organized were amazed. We had children singing songs, our quartet, and some solos.

With each program we've done since then and with the ones we're now planning, my heart fills with joy, and I find it very fulfilling and rewarding.

Of course, we are to derive pleasure from our talents and gifts. They will help us to have hope (self-expectation) and a glimpse of promises to come. I'm convinced our talents go with us on into eternity to become perfect and more complete, even as Father is perfect in *all* things.

If we are faithful in one talent, the Lord will bless us with others. ". . . that every man may improve upon his talent, that every man may gain other talents." (*Doctrine and Covenants* 82:18)

Where are the ten-talent people?

"The heights by great men reached and kept
Were not attained by sudden flight,
But they, while their companions slept
Were toiling upward in the night."
(Henry Wadsworth Longfellow)

The ten talent people are the ones balancing priorities and setting goals. They are the ones who do not run faster than they have strength or labor more than they have means. But they do *lengthen their stride* and reach beyond their grasp. They burn the midnight oil at times. They care deeply and achieve greatly. They do it because they know WHO they are. They bring honor to themselves and glory to God.

Have Patience

Patience is tied very closely to FAITH and HOPE.

It is not possible to *strengthen* faith nor *retain* hope without patience. How many times have you done the right thing and then under continued stress have broken down and given up? I have done just that and in so doing, cancelled out all the value of the effort I had given.

The Lord has said patience IS power: "And seek the face of the Lord always, that *in patience ye may possess your souls.*" (*Doctrine and Covenants* 101:30, emphasis added)

Patience is power. It will strengthen your faith, calm your spirit, sweeten your temper, enliven your hope, bury your envy, subdue your pride, and deliver you, eventually, into the life you want.

We need patience for what?—Patience to wait on the Lord and patience with ourselves.

Allowing ourselves to be scheduled on the Lord's timetable is what makes us become more like Him. He knows that it requires a time process for us to develop completely. To be impatient or to interrupt it would be like opening the oven door too soon and seeing the cake fall!

One of the purposes of tribulation is to bring us to patience. ". . . tribulation worketh patience." (Romans 5:3) And gaining patience allows us to have *needed experiences* that will be for our own good and bring us closer to Eternal Life. We wouldn't want to cheat ourselves out of one moment of this great and marvelous schooling. If you were given a scholarship to study for three weeks your favorite interest under the most acclaimed expert in that area, wouldn't you be excited? You wouldn't cheat yourself of one moment with this great tutor, whether it were cake decorating or needlework. We are here on earth for limited time, with a scholarship of mortal life, and the tutor is the Lord. We can't cheat ourselves of one minute of education.

Having patience is something I struggle for continually. I am impatient to be patient! Patience is not fatalistic or condescending. We are not to say, "Oh, well, if this is the way it is, I might as well resign to it." Elder Neal Maxwell calls it "prolonged obedience." I love that! I have to remember that all the time.

> For the natural man is an enemy to God, and has been from the fall of Adam, and will be, forever, and ever, unless he yields to the enticings of the Holy Spirit, and putteth off the natural man and becometh a saint through the atonement of Christ the Lord, and becometh as a child, submissive, meek, humble, *patient,* full of love, *willing to submit to all things which the Lord seeth fit to inflict upon him, even as a child doth submit to his father.* (Mosiah 3:19, emphasis added)

This is prolonged obedience, a willingness to submit to the will of the Lord according to HIS timetable. And to submit with meekness and humility.

As I struggled for patience with a particular adversity, my mind told me to keep going, and yet my heart was aching. The logical side kept saying to "be patient" while the emotional side was sobbing, "Isn't this enough?" Sometimes it is a real war that ensues, the greater the adversity the stronger you must battle. The secret to winning is to fight with the heart, too. In the midst of my anguish, my sweet dad read me this beautiful scripture:

> And Alma and his people did not raise their voices to the Lord their God, but did pour out their hearts to him; and he did know the thoughts of their hearts.
>
> And it came to pass that the voice of the Lord came to them in their afflictions, saying: Lift up your heads and be of good comfort for I know of the covenant which ye have made unto me; and I will covenant with my people and deliver them out of bondage.
>
> . . . *and they did submit cheerfully and with patience* to all the will of the Lord.
>
> And it came to pass that so great was their faith and their patience that the voice of the Lord came unto them again, saying: Be of good comfort, for on the morrow I will deliver you out of bondage. (Mosiah 24:12-16)

I testify to you that if we do submit cheerfully and with patience, the Lord will ease our burdens so that we cannot even feel them on our backs. They won't always be removed, but they will be lighter. He promised. Don't you just love Him for that?

In exercising patience in yourself, you must realize that *once you gain control, it takes a lot of practice to be in control one hundred percent of the time.* Perhaps it will take a lifetime of practice. I am in my middle thirties. I started to sincerely repent probably when I was about thirteen or fourteen. I have been going in to the Lord with some of the same things for over twenty years.

Just because I turned twenty or thirty didn't mean a new weakness would crop up labeled for "The Twenties" or "The Thirties." Nothing new at all, it's the same things. I can look back and see the "chipping" away as I have tried to overcome flaws, and many are beginning to have a few polished places here and there. But they are the same old rocks that have always been there. We cannot hope or *expect* to be perfect in seventy or so years. We can expect to be perfect in *some areas* in seventy or so years.

> When the veil which now encloses us is no more, time will also be no more. (See *Doctrine and Covenants* 84:100.) Even now, time is clearly not our natural dimension. Thus it is that we are never really at home in time. Alternately, we find ourselves impatiently wishing to hasten the passage of time or to hold back the dawn. We can do neither, of course. Whereas the bird is at home in the air, we are clearly not at home in time—because we belong to eternity! Time, as much as any one thing, whispers to us that we are strangers here. If time were natural to us, why is it that we have so many clocks and wear wristwatches?
>
> Thus the veil stands—not to forever shut us out—but as a reminder of God's tutoring and patient love for us. Any brush against it produces a feeling of 'not yet,' but also faint whispers of anticipation of that moment when, in the words of today's choral hymn 'Come, Let Us Anew,' those who have prevailed 'by the *patience of hope* and the labor of love' will hear the glorious words, 'Well and faithfully done; enter into my joy and sit down on my throne.' (Neal Maxwell, *Ensign,* October 1980, page 31, emphasis added)

Chapter  Four

Charity

"And now abideth faith, hope, charity, these three; but the greatest of all is charity."

1 Corinthians 13:13

Faith (love for God), Hope (love for self), and Charity (love for others)—these three qualify a person for the work, the Lord said. (*Doctrine and Covenants* 4:5) When other spiritual gifts have gone, these three shall abide together forever, said Paul. These three are inseparable; it is not possible to have one without the other, said Moroni. They are not only interrelated, they are interdependent.

> Wherefore, if a man have faith he must needs have hope; for *without faith there cannot be any hope.*
>
> And again, behold I say unto you that *he cannot have faith and hope, save he shall be meek, and lowly of heart.*
>
> . . . *and if a man be meek and lowly in heart . . . he must needs have charity;* (Moroni 7:42-44, emphasis added)

We cannot inherit the Celestial Kingdom without them. "And he commandeth all men that they must repent, and be baptized in his name, having perfect *faith* in the Holy One of Israel, or they cannot be saved in the kingdom of God." (2 Nephi 9:23, emphasis added)

> And I also remember that thou hast said that thou hast prepared a house for man, yea, even among the mansions

> of thy Father, in which man might have a more excellent hope; wherefore man must *hope* for he cannot receive an inheritance in the place which thou hast prepared.
>
> . . . And now I know that this love which thou hast had for the children of men is charity; wherefore, except men shall have *charity* they cannot inherit that place which thou hast prepared in the mansions of thy Father. (Ether 12:32, 34)

They are equally important in building the WHOLE person, the Lord said, and preparing us for Godhood.

"Behold, I will show unto the Gentiles their weakness and I will show unto them that *faith, hope,* and *charity* bringeth unto me—the fountain of all righteousness." (Ether 12:28, emphasis added)

But of the three both Paul and Moroni made it very clear that charity was the greatest.

"And now abideth faith, hope, charity, these three; *but the greatest of these is charity.*" (1 Corinthians 13:13, emphasis added)

". . . Wherefore, cleave unto charity, *which is the greatest* of all. . ." (Moroni 7:46, emphasis added)

Why would charity be the greatest of all?

Charity has been defined as love for others. A person who is without charity does not love or even care about others. The first fundamental need of every person is to be loved, the feeling of being of value to others. Then comes that need to love in return. Everyone wants and needs someone to love. Our interdependence with each other is one of the most studied facts of human reality. WE NEED EACH OTHER.

The most miserable people on earth are the ones who have not yet grasped the true understanding of their *need* to love others. It seems that unloving people are selfish. President N. Eldon Tanner observed, "The most difficult thing for us seems to be to give of ourselves, to do away with selfishness. If we really love someone, nothing is a hardship." (Conference Report, April 1967, page 104)

We have been warned that to be selfish will be commonplace

in our day.

"This know also, that in the last days perilous times shall come. For men shall be lovers of their own selves, . . ." (2 Timothy 3:1-2)

"And because iniquity shall abound, the love of many shall wax cold." (Matthew 24:12)

"And the love of men shall wax cold, . . ." (*Doctrine and Covenants* 45:27)

Selfishness means being self-centered, thinking of only yourself. It leads to self-pity which leads to resentment of others, and this leads to jealousy. Jealousy makes hearts wax cold. There is no love for others when these traits are present.

Some may think being self-centered is *too much* self-esteem. A person who is concentrating all his time, energies, and thoughts on only self is usually struggling inside to find a place of worth and value. Some place to be accepted, praised, even loved. They concentrate on themselves in hope of gaining love, when the true secret of being loved is giving love first. People with real self-esteem give little thought to their own needs.

Still, why is charity the *greatest of all?*

First Moroni described charity: "And charity suffereth long, and is kind, and envieth not, and is not puffed up, seeketh not her own, is not easily provoked, thinketh no evil, and rejoiceth not in iniquity but rejoiceth in the truth, beareth all things, believeth all things, hopeth all things, endureth all things." (Moroni 7:45)

Then he tells us why it is the greatest:

> Wherefore, my beloved brethren, *if we have not charity, ye are nothing* for charity never faileth. Wherefore, cleave unto charity, which is the greatest of all, for all things must fail—
>
> *But charity is the pure love of Christ,* and it endureth forever; *and whoso is found possessed of it at the last day, it shall be well with him.*
>
> Wherefore, my beloved brethren, pray unto the Father with all the energy of heart, that ye may be filled

with this love, which he hath bestowed upon all who are true followers of his Son, Jesus Christ; that ye may become the sons of God; *that when he shall appear we shall be like him,* for we shall see him as he is; that we may have this hope; that we may be purified even as he is pure. Amen. (Moroni 7:46-48, emphasis added)

When he said, "if ye have not charity ye are nothing," he didn't mean you are worthless. After all we have been taught that even the wicked are valued and worth a great deal to the Lord. No, he meant we would *feel* like nothing. If we don't have charity, WE WILL FEEL NO SELF-ESTEEM!

When you are serving yourself, you are selfish and self-centered. No matter how hard you try to find self-worth by focusing all efforts in your own direction, the real *feeling* of esteem never comes.

It is what the Lord meant when He said, "He that findeth his life shall lose it: and he that loseth his life for my sake shall find it." (Matthew 10:39)

When you are "finding yourself," as it is so popularly expressed, you will never gain self-esteem. But if you will lose yourself in the Lord's work, which is loving and serving others, you will "find yourself." You will have great feelings of self-worth.

A certain amount of that self-centered effort is necessary, as we have discussed in this book. We all need to take care of inner frailties. You have to begin on some level; let's call it level one. You have to restore self-worth through personal achievement and success. Not achievement and success in the eyes of the world, but in the eyes of God, particular to your own life. But you cannot stay on level one for very long. You must continue the climb higher and higher.

And where is it we are climbing? We said it already, HOME. We want to become like the Savior, like Father and Mother, and we want to go HOME.

"If ye have not charity, ye are nothing . . . charity is the *pure love* of Christ . . . whoso is found possessed of it at the last day, it shall be well with him . . . that when (Jesus Christ) shall appear we shall be *like* him . . ." (Emphasis added)

And there it is; charity is the greatest of all because it is the *pure love* of Christ. Can you describe that kind of love? Moroni tried in verse 45, but to really comprehend it, you must look at and love *every* person as though you were the Savior! If you could do that, you would "Be like Him," and that would be the "greatest of all"!

All that we have, all that with which we have been blessed, all that with which we will be blessed, are for one purpose only—to help us contribute to building up the kingdom of God. We were born to bless each other's lives.

In order to nurture charity and be able to have freedom from selfishness, resentment, or jealousy, we must:

1. Assume our responsibilities
2. Serve others

Assume Our Responsibilities

> Our life is what we make it by our own thoughts and deeds. *It is our own state and attitude of mind* which determine whether we are happy or unhappy, strong or weak, sinful or holy, foolish or wise. If one is unhappy, that state of mind belongs to himself, and is originated within himself; it is a state which responds to certain outward happenings, but its *cause* lies within, and not in those outward occurrences. If one is weak, he has brought himself to that condition by the course of thought and action *which he has chosen and is still choosing.* (James Allen, *As A Man Thinketh,* pages 17-18)

We must assume responsibility for our own thoughts and actions!

Many women write and say they have no self-esteem because of another person's abuse to them. One would say her husband tells her she's a terrible cook; another that her children said she was a horrible mother; another will say her bishop made her feel worthless; another that a neighbor keeps criticizing her home; another has a mother-in-law that ridicules her homemaking skills, etc. These unthinking, perhaps unloving individuals, who would tell you such things, cannot take away your self-esteem. No one can take away your self-esteem unless you ALLOW it to happen!

Second to your physical appearance, there is probably nothing more upsetting to your personal feelings of self-worth than negative people or circumstances in your life. At some point in everyone's life they must experience disappointment, problems, or hostility in some form or from someone. These situations cause us to develop fears and self-protective reactions. How we deal with those fears and reactions eventually produces what is our total self-image.

You can't change those things that have happened to you; there is nothing you can do about it now. What you can do now, TODAY, is start dealing squarely with the PRESENT. If you don't deal with it in a healthy manner, your self-esteem will be a low point.

What does dealing squarely with the present mean? It means controlling what YOU CAN CONTROL! Control means to *change* those negative aspects of your personality that are causing your poor self-image. In order to change, you must assume responsibility for your own thoughts and actions. When we aren't assuming responsibility, we are blaming or excusing our behavior on anything except our own thoughts.

1. *Blaming family or environment.* "It's my family's fault." "I came from the wrong side of the tracks." "What do you expect from me? Look at my family." "People reject me because I'm poor."

2. *Blaming events.* "I only have bad luck." "Sure she's a success; she's lucky." "The weather prevented me from doing it."

3. *Labeling.* "I am a lonely person." "I am a depressed person." I had a roommate in college that started every

morning with the statement, "Oh, I am so depressed." She made me depressed. Whether we label ourselves or accept someone else's label of us, we are using a crutch.

4. *Blaming others.* "He hurt me." "The bishop fouled it up." "She insulted me, so I quit."
5. *Excusing our behavior.* "I was born this way." "This is inherited. My mom is just like this." "Well, everybody else does it." "Satan made me do it." "I am not organized." "I was sick."

If you can't solve problems, if you can't deal with conflict or instigate change, your self-esteem is going to stay low. You will not love yourself, and you will not be able to love God or others to the most full measure of charity. *You will be out of control, and when that happens, you have the overwhelming feeling that circumstances are controlling you.*

Some time ago some relatives of a young woman I know came to see her because they "could no longer go on living this way," they said. They had the need, they said, to make her aware of how much misery she was causing in their lives. What proceeded to happen was a most crushing experience for her. I share this with you so there will not be any doubt that the message of assuming responsibility is critical.

As they sat around a table, they told her that her weaknesses were making them unhappy. They were miserable because of her character flaws. They then described what it was she was doing that they could no longer stand. They described accurately many of her weaknesses.

But then they began to judge her. They looked at her life, her goals, ambitions, and achievements, and they judged her motivation. They believed she was motivated by power and money. She struggled desperately in between her sobs to tell them that they were wrong. She tried hard to tell them how she felt and thought.

Instead of listening, they accused her of being "past feeling" and unteachable. They had prayed and felt "good" about what they were saying. Their words had crushed her, but now they said something that broke her spirit. They told her to repent and pray that the Holy Ghost would return to her. They knew she did not have the Spirit.

She returned home, hardly able to walk in the house. She literally collapsed in her husband's arms. She sobbed for hours. He tried to comfort her. As the hours went on, she felt worse and worse. "They must be right," she thought. "They said they had prayed. Maybe I don't have the Spirit. Oh, my Father, how could I have fallen so low? How could I have been so insensitive to losing the Spirit? How could I have let my personality hurt others so much? I must be all they say I am; there were four of them and one of me."

Morning finally came. Her husband told her how much he loved her. He told her of all her positive points. He told her that he felt those relatives were jealous. He tried his best to comfort her. In other trials she found comfort with him because the two of them were *sharing* the trial. But on this occasion she was truly alone. He could not come where she was at that moment.

At this point, she told me she felt in complete darkness. She couldn't do anything except lay on her bed, doubting *all* that her life had been. She wondered how she could have gotten so far off course. She questioned all those experiences in her life that she thought were spiritual. She was filled with self-doubt, self-pity, and for the first time in her life—despair. She had never known despair until that moment.

Finally, in the late afternoon, no longer able to stand it, she went into her closet and poured out her heart to our Father in Heaven. She begged for forgiveness. She begged Him to help her see the errors of her life. She pleaded with Him to spare her family, her children, from her weaknesses and flaws. If necessary, take her now; she could not bear to cause anymore anguish in anyone's lives.

Then she said, "As I got up and went back to my bed, I was suddenly aware of all the sunbeams in the room. As that happened, I was filled with the most *intense* warmth and encompassed by a flooding feeling of love. I knew it to be the love of Father. The despair began to diminish. Then came the moving and gentle reproach—chastisement that quieted the self-pity. The message was loud and clear—'*in order to influence many, we can't help but offend a few.*'" She explained to me that then came the understanding that eliminated the self-doubt. She realized they were judging her according to their thoughts. She realized that "we perceive people and their actions according to the way *we* would do it or think about." At that moment it was clear why they had said what they did. She also realized these things were coming to her *by the Spirit.* He was not gone from her life!

It was also clear that she had already known her weaknesses. They weren't telling her anything new. But their perception of her efforts, goals, and achievements had been from *where they were.* The Lord will reveal our weaknesses to us so that we can improve, but we are to concentrate on only our own, not other's.

> And why beholdest thou the mote that is in thy brother's eye, but considerest not the beam that is in thine own eye?
>
> Or how wilt thou say to thy brother, Let me pull out the mote out of thine eye; and behold, a beam is in thine own eye? (Matthew 7:3-4)

> This should leave no doubt in any mind. The unequalness of the beam and the mote is telling. A mote is a tiny sliver like a small portion from a toothpick, while the beam is usually a great, strong timber or metal which runs from wall to wall to support the heavy roof of the building. When one is loaded down with the beam-size weaknesses and sins, it is certainly wrong to forget his own difficult position while he makes mountains of the molehill-size errors of his brother. (Spencer W. Kimball, *Miracle of Forgiveness,* page 269)

It was a bittersweet experience. She learned from this experience many valuable lessons. The most important was on assuming our responsibilities. If everything they had said about her was true, she could not make their lives miserable. Only they can do that. They were responsible for their own thoughts and actions. And in reverse, they could not take away her self-esteem. Only she could choose to let that happen. Self-esteem is a *choice*. And it's not a choice we make once, but one we will make over and over again throughout life. Some people think being secure in your identity or having a good self-image means your skin is "thick." Or that if you feel good about yourself, you should be immune to the pricks and barbs of others. That's simply not true. You are a human being with a heart as well as a mind. It hurts to be scorned, abused, or degraded. But we must press on. *Choose* to have a good self-image and *choose* to replace negative thoughts with positive ones. It is a choice we must make many times in life because there will always be adverse people and circumstances around us. It seems the more you succeed the more threatened some around you will become and would seek to hurt you.

Someone said once, "The weak can be joked out of anything but their weakness." We are probably most angry when we are confronted by our weaknesses. When the Lord chastens, He does so by the Spirit. When the Holy Ghost is present, we have such a reproving we are *inspired*, ready to go out and conquer ourselves. If the Spirit isn't present, the feeling of being suppressed (and despair) becomes prominent. And so it should be in dealing with one another.

So often we abuse the scripture that tells us, "And if thy brother or sister offend thee, thou shalt take him or her between him or her and thee alone; and if he or she confess thou shalt be reconciled." (*Doctrine and Covenants* 42:88) We should settle our differences, peacefully, between us, but that doesn't mean hand the other person a list of their weaknesses. It means we should go to the other in a spirit of humility and forgiveness.

Forgiveness is a hard principle. I am always touched and inspired by the example of those around me who teach me to be forgiving. For me it has been a hard principle to learn. And I haven't *learned* it (or anything) yet. I am still working on it.

I had the opportunity for a lesson on forgiveness. Although I cannot share the experience with you, I can share the message. My mind recalled what the Lord said about forgiveness:

> Wherefore, I say unto you, that ye ought to forgive one another; for he that forgiveth not his brother his trespasses standeth condemned before the Lord; for there remaineth in him the greater sin.
>
> I, the Lord, will forgive whom I will forgive, but of you it is *required* to forgive all men. (*Doctrine and Covenants* 64:9-10, emphasis added)

He didn't say "it would be nice" if you would forgive, or "I encourage" you to forgive, or "I invite" you to forgive. He said "of you it is REQUIRED."

And then in Alma 41:12-15:

> And now behold, is the meaning of the word restoration to take a thing of a natural state and place it in an unnatural state, or to place it in a state opposite to its nature?
>
> O, My son, this is not the case; but the meaning of the word restoration is to bring back again evil for evil, or carnal for carnal, or devilish for devilish—good for that which is good; righteous for that which is righteous; just for that which is just; merciful for that which is merciful.
>
> Therefore, my son, see that you are merciful unto your brethren; deal justly, judge righteously, and do good continually! and if ye do all these things then shall ye receive your reward; yea, ye shall have mercy restored unto you again; ye shall have justice restored unto you again; ye shall have a righteous judgment restored unto you again; and ye shall have good rewarded unto you again.
>
> *For that which ye do send out shall return unto you again, and be restored;* therefore, the word restoration more fully condemneth the sinner, and justifieth him not at all.

How can we ask forgiveness if we don't forgive? How can we develop *real* charity, the *pure* love of Christ if we don't forgive?

It isn't always easy. For me I realized the bottom line was

pride. My pride had been hurt. To forgive sometimes is like taking a huge bite of a prickly pear cactus and swallowing it whole!

I discovered one more thing. Your mind and reasoning can be taught and arrive there before your heart does. That's okay. If we'll just begin to ACT on a principle, the commitment and love for it *will* come. James Allen called it the "as if" principle. If you will just act "as if" a quality exists, it will begin to develop. Your heart will catch up to your reason.

Taking a bite of the prickly pear cactus is exactly what is required. Remember how Moroni described charity:

"And charity suffereth long, and is kind, and envieth not, and is not puffed up, seeketh not her own, is not easily provoked," (Moroni 7:45)

It is *our responsibility* to forgive and get along with others. If everyone of us were doing that, would there be any differences among us? If we were each concentrating on the beam in our own eyes, would we ever see the mote in another's? If we had a crystal that saw into the good of each other's hearts, would we love one another more?

UNDERSTANDING
If I knew you and you knew me,
　　If both of us could clearly see,
And with an inner sight divine
　　The meaning of your heart and mine,
I'm sure that we would differ less,
　　And clasp our hands in friendliness;
Our thoughts would pleasantly agree
　　If I knew you and you knew me.
　　　　　　　　　　—Nixon Waterman

The way we treat others or think of others is the way we feel about ourselves. We have to assume the responsibility for that.

It feels so good to gossip or criticize others when we feel inadequate. It assures us they aren't perfect. When we look for the faults in others, it soothes our knowledge of the weaknesses we live with daily.

What we do or say is a reflection of how we feel or what we have thought. When you speak of others or to others, what are you saying about yourself?

A sister wrote me this letter:

> My wonderful husband and I just celebrated our fifth wedding anniversary with NO children, and we have encountered many judgmental comments from people over the years. A prime example occurred several years ago at a Relief Society meeting on "Making Mealtime Enjoyable." I mentioned during the course of the lesson that my husband and I often listen to soft music while we eat, and sometimes we light candles at the dinner table. Afterwards, one sister asked me why we didn't have any children yet, if we were so romantic. Needless to say, I felt some bitterness creep into my soul, and I didn't attend Relief Society again for awhile after that. But then, as I analyzed the situation, I realized that that sister may have been feeling some jealousy towards me because she has seven children to care for, and I have none.
>
> At any rate, we have learned to cope with the inability to conceive a child and with the untactful comments. We try to fill our lives with other meaningful things and experiences, realizing that the Lord still loves us and has great things in store for us, if we remain faithful.

Can you see what the woman with seven children was saying about herself? And in a positive light, can you see how the other sister assumed responsibility for how she would react and feel?

Service alone is not enough. We must place all our heart's (emotions) might (will), mind (thoughts), and strength (time) in developing charity. We must *look* for the good in others. We must be happy with the success of others. We must speak well of one another.

"I do not know of *anything* that will contribute more to *unity* in a ward, in a state, in a country, than for members to speak well of each other." (President David O. McKay, emphasis added)

I remember being taught the concept, "If you don't have anything good to say about someone, don't say anything at all." That is a false attitude. The Savior's principle is, "If you don't have anything good to say about someone, GET RID of those feelings!"

I find it hard to like everyone. There always seem to be some people who are self-centered or arrogant. Loving others may be easier than liking them. I love my children, but I don't like everything they do. I love Sister Kimball's honest evaluation of her own feelings:

> You know, in all my life I really disliked only one person. It was a woman I could hardly stand to speak to. She was so sickly sweet, yet so self-centered. She had nothing to talk about except her husband and her children's great accomplishments. She had no life of her own and had such vanity in the reflected glory. I find I cannot recall her without distaste. May the Lord forgive me. (*Camilla*, page 189)

Well, what are we to do? In Sister Kimball's own words, ". . . may the Lord forgive [us]." If we keep working on it, if we keep repenting, if we keep trying to find at least *one good point* in everyone, we will begin to slowly discover what Moroni meant by PURE Love of Christ.

Repentance is as much a turning *towards the good* as it is turning away from the evil!

We must assume our responsibility to repent. There is a prevalent feeling that repentance is for only those who commit gross sins. If we are desirous of living the gospel, we must come to think of repentance in all we do that is offensive to God, especially in all we do (or don't do) that stifles charity. The Lord wants us to come to Him in repentance. He will then help us in *getting rid* of all our adverse behaviors.

> He wants us to come to him as we are. We do not have to be perfect to go to him . . . The Lord loves us and wants us to overcome our sins, and He will help us

as we exercise our free agency. We must initiate the process of repentance and strive with all of our might to overcome our weaknesses. (Joseph F. Smith)

There is one more area to mention in assuming our responsibilities: sharing the Priesthood.

The priesthood and women cannot really be separated. 'The priesthood is without father, without mother, . . . having neither beginning of days, nor end of life.' (Hebrews 7:3) Nor maleness nor femaleness. It is head to them both. Male and female alike come under it and must understand their true relationship to it, one to serve as priest within it, the other eventually as a priestess. Men here are given the priesthood power, but both man and woman must bring themselves into submission unto it, rather than she unto him as a person. The man must assume the same relationship of honor and obedience to priesthood truths and doctrines that the woman does. That is, it precedes them both. For the man to assume that because he 'holds' the priesthood that it is his or that he is somehow exalted in importance is a serious distortion:

'That they may be conferred upon us, it is true; but when we undertake to cover our sins, or to gratify our pride, our vain ambition, or to exercise control or dominion or compulsion . . . in any degree of unrighteousness, behold, the heavens withdraw themselves!' (*Doctrine and Covenants* 121:37)

There is no chauvinism in true righteousness. . .Justice, fairness, sensitivity, and respect—regardless of another's sex—reflect the depth and maturity of the commitment of a priesthood bearer.

For a mortal to attempt to use the priesthood without honor and righteousness is to attempt that which even God cannot do. Priesthood bearers must become men of virtue. *Men and women alike have this commandment and promise:*

'Let thy bowels also be full of charity towards all men, and to the household of faith, and let virtue garnish thy thoughts unceasingly; *then shall thy confidence wax strong* in the presence of God; and the doctrine of the priesthood shall distill upon thee as the dews from heaven.' (*Doctrine and Covenants* 121:45, *Ensign*, September 1980, page 19)

Women must be accountable for their priesthood responsibilities: Those are:

1. Realizing it has been given to man as a Divine order of authority from God—a stewardship.
2. Its power is available to any woman, whether the priesthood is in her home or not.
3. Our callings from the Lord are priesthood callings.
4. By submitting to the priesthood, in righteousness, we are participating in our part of the plan of salvation.
5. We have the power to call upon spiritual (priesthood) gifts for our personal use and for the benefit of our families.
6. The male cannot gain salvation without the female.
7. Our priesthood partners cannot grow or develop to full potential unless enhanced by female spirituality and support.

God created man in His image, we are taught. What does that mean? What is the image of God? "And I, God, created man in mine own image . . . male and female created I them." (Moses 2:27)

The image of God is a MAN AND A WOMAN. No, God is not both a man and a woman; there is another person, a partner, His wife. The image of God or Godhood is this partnership. "Neither is the man without the woman, neither the woman without the man . . ." (1 Corinthians 11:11)

President Kimball has elaborated on this scripture in a way that only a prophet can:

> And the scripture says, 'And I, God said unto mine Only Begotten, which was with me from the beginning; Let us make man (not a separate man, but a complete man, which is husband and wife) in our image, after our likeness; and it was so.' (Moses 2:26) What a beautiful partnership!
>
> 'Male and female created he *them*; and blessed *them*,

and called *their* name Adam (Mr. and Mrs. Adam, I suppose, or Brother and Sister Adam) in the day when they were created.' (Genesis 5:1-2) This is a partnership. (*Ensign*, March 1976, page 71)

There are some sisters who ponder the administrative structure of the Church and trouble themselves with what they think they don't have without ever coming to a full understanding of their own special and unique mission and the great blessings reserved specifically for them. We hear it expressed in terms that suggest that because women don't have the priesthood they are shortchanged.

There are still others of our sisters who have the mis-understanding that priesthood is synonymous with men, and so they excuse themselves and have no concern for studying its importance in their own lives. The term priesthood is used without qualification, whether it is referring to a bearer of the priesthood, priesthood bless-ings, or priesthood ordinances. Our hearts should cry out in either case, and we should raise our voices and shout warnings to sisters whose dreams are built on such faulty foundations.

Our greatest dreams will be fulfilled only as we come to understand fully and experience the blessings of the priesthood in our own lives. If we were to begin with the time a child is given a name and a blessing and then continue on through baptism, confirmation, the sacrament, callings and being set apart, patriarchal bless-ings, administrations, the endowment, and finally celestial marriage, we would quickly realize that all the saving blessings of the priesthood are for boys and girls, men and women. And while that divine mission of mother-hood is paramount, it is not all-inclusive. To help another gain eternal life is a companion privilege. This privilege, indeed this sacred responsibility, this noblest of callings, is *denied to no worthy person.* (Ardeth Kapp, *Blue-prints for Living*, Volume 1, page 83, emphasis added)

Some inborn characteristics and qualities are uniquely feminine. God designed it that way. There were no mistakes in Heaven. Women have a definite responsibility to not only retain those specific feminine characteristics and qualities but to add to them—to leave this world having made their personal environment better than what they had found it.

"As the bow unto the cord is
So unto the man is woman.
Though she bends him, she obeys him,
Though she draws him, yet she follows;
Useless each without the other."

—Henry Wadsworth Longfellow

Love is the power upon which the Priesthood operates. It is love that gives us the power to lead and influence others, not control, but influence. "No power or influence can or ought to be maintained by virtue of the priesthood, only by persuasion, by long-suffering, by gentleness and meekness, and by love unfeigned;" (*Doctrine and Covenants* 121:41)

GOD IS LOVE.

Give Service

"Love in your heart wasn't put there to stay;
Love isn't love, till you give it away."

Oscar Hammerstein III (Sound of Music)

For me, a great experience has been to "transport" myself to the upper room where the Savior ate his last meal. Those must have been tender moments for Him. He knew what was coming in a few hours. He had been hated and persecuted, rejected by His own people. He was spending His last hours on earth with His dearest friends. They had been His companions almost constantly for at least a year, perhaps longer. Day and night they had walked and talked, sharing each other's lives. They had eaten meals with Him, shared shelter and warmth; they had knelt in prayer with Him. He taught the glorious truths of who they were, where they came from, why they were there, and where they could expect to go. He had poured out all his knowledge and blessings upon them. They must have wept and laughed together as brothers. He loved them.

As they shared that last evening together, I like to imagine that the Savior spent a few special minutes with each of His beloved apostles. He might have given each a particular word of encouragement. I know He must have expressed His love individually and personally. To Peter He may have embraced him and whispered, "You are so valiant; upon you have I built my church." To Matthew, "You have such a strong spirit; lead well, my friend." Maybe to Timothy he said, "Thank you for all your support; I love you." And to John, "Beloved, I trust you with my mother; I love you, my brother."

I sense from reading the account of His last supper that He made it a most important occasion for *them*. Can you imagine that? If you knew that you were going to be tried, mocked, beaten, flesh torn, and crucified in a matter of hours, where would your thoughts be?

After they had eaten, "Jesus knowing that the Father had given all things into his hands, and that he was come from God, and went to God; He riseth from supper, and laid aside his garments; and took a towel, and girded himself." (John 13:3-4)

The Son of God then did a most condescending act. The total selfless love that He expressed at that moment tenders my soul: "After that he poureth water into a basin, and began to wash the disciples' feet, and to wipe them with the towel wherewith he was girded."

It was through this washing that they covenanted with each other. Do you know what that covenant was?

> So after he had washed their feet, and had taken his garments, and was set down again, he said unto them, Know ye what I have done to you?
>
> Ye call me Master and Lord; and ye say well; for so I am.
>
> If I then, your Lord and Master, have washed your feet; ye also ought to wash one another's feet.
>
> For I have given you an example, that ye should do as I have done to you.

> Verily, verily, I say unto you, The servant is not greater than his lord; neither he that is sent greater than he that sent him. (John 13:12-16)

And then He promised them how they would feel about life and themselves if they kept the covenant: "If ye know these things, happy are ye if ye do them." (John 13:17)

Then, with words that have come to stir my whole being, Jesus Christ said: "A new commandment I give unto you, That ye love one another; as I have loved you, that ye also love one another. By this shall all men know that ye are my disciples, if ye have love one to another." (John 13:34-35)

Some people believe that charity is service. It is not. It is *through service* we can develop charity. In nurturing charity within ourselves there is the hope (expectation) that we can become as Jesus Christ himself. It is the *only* way. Why else would it be "the greatest of all"? How can you become like the Savior if you don't *know* Him, and how can you *know* Him if you don't do the things He did?

> And beside this, giving all diligence, add to your faith virtue; and to virtue knowledge;
>
> And to knowledge temperance; and to temperance patience; and to patience godliness;
>
> And to godliness brotherly kindness; and to brotherly kindness charity.
>
> For if these things be in you, and abound, they make you that ye shall neither be barren nor unfruitful in the knowledge of our Lord Jesus Christ. (2 Peter 1:5-8)

Peter listed many of the things we talked about in this book, starting with faith, virtue (strength or courage), knowledge, temperance (self-control), patience, godliness (seek spiritual gifts, repent, etc.), and brotherly kindness (service) which will all bring us to charity (the pure love of Christ). If these things are in you, you shall "Neither be barren nor unfruitful in the knowledge of our Lord Jesus Christ."

There have been those of whom I have read about or known, that because of their great selfless service, they have developed much charity. Perhaps some have even tasted what it means to have "the pure love of Christ."

It was my privilege to grow up in New England, in Concord, Massachusetts. There was the birthplace of our nation, the beginnings of a place wherein the gospel could be restored. Ours was a land that had been consecrated for a special purpose. The Lord had prepared men to bring forth this nation (as recorded in 2 Nephi 13).

There was one among them named Nathan Hale. At age twenty, Nathan Hale caught *the Spirit* and vision of the American Revolution, and he volunteered as a soldier. He quickly distinguished himself as a valiant leader and won a place for himself in a group called The Rangers. The Rangers were respected for their fighting qualities and leadership on dangerous missions.

General George Washington asked the Rangers for a volunteer to infiltrate enemy lines and obtain information on British position. Nathan Hale stepped forward.

He was successful in gaining the secrets. But the day he tried to cross over to American lines, he was betrayed by his cousin and captured. With taunting remarks about his having his whole life ahead of him to live, he was given the opportunity to renounce his American Allegiance. But it was with great charity that Nathan must have sensed it was not his life alone. He must have realized that he represented every young man and woman giving their life for God, country, and each other. Nathan loved his country and his countrymen. It was with great charity that he went to the gallows that hour and said, "I regret only that I have but one life to lose for my country."

Then there was another patriot named Patrick Henry. Benjamin Franklin called him the "greatest orator and statesman of the time." Patrick Henry was a powerful and influential man in the Colonies. He was married to his childhood sweetheart Sarah. Patrick could have risen to much greater powers and influence, but he held himself back. He did so because his wife Sarah became seriously mentally ill. In that era the mentally ill were thought to have committed some hidden sin for which they were being punished. They were committed to bacteria infested dungeons, chained to their beds, and left to die of tuberculosis or infection.

Patrick could have freed himself of his obligation to Sarah. No one would have blamed him. He could have been free to pursue his political ambitions to the fullest. Benjamin Franklin believed he would be President one day.

But he put aside his personal gain to care for and attend to the needs of his confined and ailing wife. He loved her to the very end. Of Patrick Henry it has been said that he suffered for his lovely wife, imprisoned in her own mind. It was with great *empathy*, besides conviction, he delivered those famous words to the Virginia Convention, "Give me liberty, or give me death!"

Henry Wadsworth Longfellow from his youth was destined for success. He was an author, professor, and poet. He was a world celebrity and a wealthy man. He had a beautiful marriage and six lovely children. At the height of his career and success, he suffered a great personal tradgedy.

His wife Frances was melting sealing wax which caught on fire. Trying to extinguish the flames, her dress went up in flames, and she screamed for his help. By the time he reached her it was too late, and she died. He was so tortured from the memory of her screaming and agonizing burns that he went to his bed and desired to die. He felt he could no longer go on without her. One evening his family gathered together in his room, possibly to bid their father farewell.

He later wrote that when he looked up from his sick bed and into the faces of those children, he saw a legacy to his wife. He knew it was not his life alone. He knew he must get up and love them and serve them all the rest of his life. He did. He walked and talked and played with them. He was both father and mother, and it was in those years he wrote his masterpiece, "The Children's Hour," which clearly tells of his love of family life. Henry Wadsworth Longfellow, acclaimed author and poet, knew the meaning of charity.

Then there was brother Willard Richards, a successful physician. He became a frequent traveling companion to the Prophet Joseph Smith. He was with him as the Prophet preached the gospel, visited the saints, and defended himself against persecutors. He went with the Prophet to Carthage jail:

> While in the jail, the jailor, named Stigall, suggested they would be safer in the cell. Joseph said, 'After supper we will go in.' Mr. Stigall went out, and Joseph said to Dr. Richards, 'If we go into the cell, will you go in with us?' The doctor answered, 'Brother Joseph, you did not ask me to cross the river with you—you did not ask me to come to Carthage—and you did not ask me to come to jail with you—and do you think I would forsake you now?'

And then with great love for the Prophet, I know Willard Richards had charity when he continued and said:

> 'But I will tell you what I will do; if you are condemned to be hung for treason, I will be hung in your stead, and you shall go free.' Joseph said, 'You cannot.' And the doctor replied, 'I will.' (*History of the Church,* Volume VI, page 616)

There was charity in the heart of a lovely young English girl born to a wealthy family in the Nineteenth Century. Her home was filled with nobility, and she was taught in the best schools and learned all the social graces. In her heart she enjoyed caring for visiting babies or caring for sick farmers on her father's estate more than going to parties. She saved the life of an old shepherd's dog when its broken leg had condemned it to death.

When she was sixteen, she made a decision to devote herself to the service of others. She did not yet know, however, how to do this. Several years later she became interested in studying health and reforms for the poor and suffering. This was unheard of for a wealthy girl. Hospitals were dirty and unmanaged. Her father threatened to disown her. But her heart had grown tender for the suffering she saw around her.

She went to serve her countrymen fighting in the Crimea. Upon arriving, she found the hospital was a dirty barracks with no cots, no food, or medical supplies. The wounded lay bleeding on the floors. She immediately set people cleaning, doing kitchen work, while she set up a nursing schedule and proper diets.

Nursing had been a disreputable profession. Doctors and officials resented the reforms this earnest and sincere woman was trying to do. It was an uphill battle. But she won them over, and Florence Nightingale is known as the "Mother of Nursing." She said, "I serve because I love."

Then there were three young men named Brother Huntington, Brother Grant, and Brother Kimball. I know they knew the pure love of Christ. They were part of a relief party who went to the aid of the Martin Handcart Company. They were all only eighteen years of age.

> On this trip they faced a stream that was swollen with ice and snow. Have you ever walked, even to the knee level, through such water? The pioneers almost hopelessly stood back, unable to go through in their weakened and emaciated condition. Those three boys carried *everyone* of the company across and then crossed back, sometimes in water up to their waists. All three died from exposure. (Truman Madsen, *Highest in Us*, page 54)

There are some of you who suffer from loneliness. Many of the sisters are single, having never been married, widowed, or divorced. There is absolutely no way to prevent those moments from feeling alone, but no one ever need be lonely!

Looking back on the year and a half I was divorced, I see my total responsibility for the moments I wallowed in loneliness. Whenever I reflect on the times in my life that were lonely, I see that I was turning my thoughts inward.

A wise sister said: "I need to be reminded of the dangers of turning inward, of grabbing too tightly to my own soul. In trying to preserve myself, I would squeeze all of the life out of myself. There are grave dangers in considering too prominently our own desires and needs which strangle the opportunity to look beyond ourselves."

Whenever we see others who suffer from loneliness, we can usually find a life empty of service and love for others. A lot of women believe if they aren't married, for whatever reason, or don't have children, that they might as well settle back and wait out their mortal existence.

President Harold B. Lee said:

> Those without mates—some of you do not now have a companion in your home. Some of you have lost your husband, or you may not yet have found a companion. . . *Life holds so much for you.* Take *strength* in meeting your challenges. There are so many ways to find fulfillment, in *serving* those who are dear to you, in *doing well* the tasks that are before you in your employment or in your home. The Church offers so much opportunity for you—*TO HELP SOULS*—beginning with your own, to find the joy of eternal life. . . Do not let self-pity or despair beckon you from the course you know is right. *Turn your thoughts to helping others . . . (Strengthening the Home,* emphasis added)

It is a mistake for women to believe that life for them begins with marriage and children. A woman can (and must) have a useful life all on her own. A woman must feel important and worthwhile, regardless of her "social" status or physical limitations!

Helen Keller should be an inspiration to women everywhere, handicapped either physically or by their own weaknesses! Inspiration is the wrong word to describe her. She is a ROCK. I love her because of her life. What prompted my interest in Helen Keller was a picture of her in the encyclopedia. When I saw it, I was astonished by the look on her face. She did not look blind. There was a definite sparkle in her eyes, a look of depth, intelligence, and recognition. Eyes are the reflection of the soul. Every ounce of her soul was reflected in her eyes and in her whole face. As I read books about her work and thoughts and accomplishments, I felt her indomitable spirit, her enthusiasm for life, her refusal to let her handicaps affect her stay on earth. She was responsible for much of the improvement of life for the blind. She graduated from Radcliffe with honors. She was active on the staffs of many foundations for the blind and deaf. She travelled to underdeveloped and war-ravaged countries and helped establish better conditions there for the blind. She lectured in America and in twenty-five other countries. She aided and comforted servicemen who had been blinded in World War II. She wrote many books which have been translated into more than fifty languages. Wherever she went, she brought new courage to thousands of blind persons and inspired millions of others with her zeal. She never married; she never had any children, but she influenced literally millions.

She could have said, "I'm deaf, dumb, and blind. What can I do? Who can I help?" She could even have said, "Why me? Others *owe* it to give me help." But, no! Helen Keller thought the opposite. She had love in her heart for others because she served them. And the world loved her in return. She knew the word charity. Helen Keller—blind, deaf, and dumb—said, "I have found life so beautiful!"

Napolean had everything in the world—glory, power, and riches. But he served only himself. He once wrote, "I have never known six happy days in my life."

There is a Primary teacher I know, a single sister with a family to support, who is developing charity. She takes a personal interest in every child that comes into her care. She was my daughter's Primary teacher two years ago. There were always notes sent home with words to build self-esteem. "You looked pretty today." "That was a good prayer." "Thank you for being so reverent." Birthdays were never forgotten. In September every child received a little bag stuffed with pencils, cute stickers, and all sorts of good things for school. Holidays were always celebrated with a little token. Then there were the notes that came to the house—what child isn't thrilled with personal mail, a note of encouragement and love from their Primary teacher. Even now, two years later, this teacher still has a warm word for every child that has been in her class. She's sowing seeds of pure love.

A young man who lives in one of the stakes here in Las Vegas was assigned to be deacon's advisor. The quorum had nine boys, six of whom were inactive. He made a commitment to himself to activate all six boys. Weeks passed; nothing was happening despite his repeated phone calls and visits. Finally he realized the reason. "If I am to serve them, I must love them. If I am to love them, I must serve them." So with his own money he bought an old car. He went to each boy (all nine) and told them that if they would fix the car up each Saturday morning, they could eventually sell it. The money would go for a trip to Disneyland for them all.

So Saturday after Saturday the boys would come. He would always be there for them. Sometimes eight would show up, sometimes five, sometimes one, and sometimes none. Saturday after Saturday of fellowship and love. Within a few months he activated all but one boy. The boy had never come out.

I know this leader was developing charity as he recommitted himself to serve and love this deacon. One Sunday instead of calling, he drove to the boy's house and knocked on the door. A sleepy thirteen-year-old opened the door. The leader invited him to church. He declined. The next Sunday he persisted. The boy declined and so on for several weeks. Then one Sunday the boy answered the door and said, "Okay, I'll go this once to get you off my back."

The next Sunday the advisor drove up and instead of knocking he honked. After some honking, he went up and knocked on the door. The boy was half-dressed but was getting ready.

Sunday after Sunday passed with the advisor driving up and honking. At first the young deacon came down the sidewalk buttoning a shirt or combing his hair. Before long the boy started coming out of the house all dressed at the first honk of the horn. Then, imagine how the advisor's heart swelled inside with love, as one Sunday he turned the corner and saw this deacon waiting on the curb.

After some months passed, a Sunday came when the boy wasn't waiting on the curb. The advisor worried; maybe he was ill. Real love had grown for this boy. He walked to the door, but before he could knock it opened. There stood his deacon dressed for church with a big smile. "I won't be going with you, Brother _____; today I'm taking my dad."

Elder Vaughn Featherstone remembers how the pure love of others comforted him as a child and helped him into the gospel.

> At about that same time we couldn't afford much clothing either. I had a pair of shoes that I'd wear to church. They weren't the best shoes. They had holes in the bottom sole, so I'd cut out pieces of cardboard and slide them in as an insole. When I went to church, I would sit with both feet flat on the floor; I didn't want to raise a leg and have someone see 'Quaker Oats' across the bottom of my shoe. I'd go off to church that way, and everything was fine until those shoes wore out. Then I didn't know what I would do. I remember it was Saturday, and I thought, 'I've got to go to church. Over at church I am somebody. They really care about me.' I remember thinking that through, and I went to a little box of shoes some neighbors had given us. I went through them, but I could find only one pair of shoes that would fit me. They were a pair of nurses' shoes. I thought, 'How can I wear those? They'll laugh me to scorn over at church.' And so I decided I wouldn't wear them, and I wouldn't go to church.
>
> I went through that night, and the next morning I knew I had to go! I had to wear the nurses' shoes. There was a great attraction over at church. I had to go. I decided what to do. I would run over there very early and sit down close to the front before anybody got there. I thought, 'I'll put my feet back under the pew so no one can see them, and then I'll wait till everyone leaves. After they're gone, I'll come running home half an hour later or something.' That was my plan. I dashed over to church half an hour early, and it worked. Nobody was there. I

put my feet back under the bench. Pretty soon everyone came in, and then all of a sudden someone announced: 'We will now separate for classes.' I had forgotten we had to go to class. I was terrified! The ushers came down the aisle, and as they got to our row, everybody got up and left. But I just sat there. I couldn't move. I knew I couldn't move for fear someone would see my shoes. The pressure was intense. That whole meeting seemed to stop and wait until I moved, so I had to move. I got up and followed the class downstairs.

I think I learned the greatest lesson I have ever learned in my life that day. I went downstairs to class, and the teacher had us sit in a big half-circle. Each of my shoes felt two feet in diameter. I can't tell you how embarrassed I was. I watched, but do you know, not one of those eight and nine year old children in that class laughed at me. Not one of them looked at me. No one pointed at my shoes. My teacher didn't look. I was watching everyone to see if anyone was looking at me, and I didn't hear a word of the lesson. When it was finally over I dashed home, went in the house, and thought to myself, 'Thank goodness nobody saw them.' How ridiculous! Of course they saw those nurses' shoes that I had to wear to church. But they had the fine instinct not to laugh. (Featherstone, *Charity Never Faileth*)

My father had no shoes often in his life either. In the middle of winter one year, when he was about eight years old, his shoes gave out. He had patched and roped them together for the last time. It was a bitter, cold school day, and his mother told him to stay home. It was a five-mile walk each way. Saturday would bring him another pair of shoes she hoped.

My father said he, too, HAD to go. At school he was learning great things; at school he could make things happen. So he started his walk in the freezing cold.

Along the way he met his friend, Tomas. Tomas questioned him as to why he would go to school with no shoes in that weather. My father told him that his feet ached, but his heart ached more. I know that little children are filled with more pure love than we can ever imagine. I know it was with charity that Tomas said, "Alex, you carry my books, and I will carry you." And so he did. One little burden on another's back, five miles each way.

I have no idea where Tomas is or who he is, but he inspired me. And I am so grateful he helped my father keep his commitments to himself. Keeping those commitments helped shape a slum child's life. And I am so grateful to my father for all the times he has "carried" me on his back. He has done it with the pure love of Christ.

And I know President Kimball knows the meaning of charity. President Kimball IS charity.

Several years ago he and Sister Kimball were invited to a dinner at the BYU President's home. Many of the faculty and staff were present. President and Sister Kimball arrived in a car, driven by a chauffeur, because the President doesn't drive anymore. The chauffeur parked and waited in the car.

After all the greetings were over, everyone stepped aside so that President and Sister Kimball could serve themselves first. An observer said he watched with anticipation what the prophet would choose; he'd heard he didn't eat much.

Sister Kimball went first and then the President came, plate in hand, silverware tucked under it, and a roll in his forearm. He piled the plate higher and higher. Then carefully balancing it all, including a glass of punch, he guided Camilla to her seat. Then others present saw pure love. The prophet of God went out the front door, down the walk, and served the chauffeur first!

President Kimball is a Celestial teacher. I don't remember the General Authority that talked about being telestial, terrestrial, and celestial teachers, but I do remember he said that the main body of the Church was at a terrestrial level. That means we serve, we offer "brotherly kindness" as Peter called it, for ourselves. We feel good about our acts of service, we feel accomplishment. As we learn line upon line, precept upon precept, we need to experience those feelings of being worthwhile and accomplishing. We need to feel the pleasure of the Lord. But we can't stay there! We need to use our service as a vehicle to move on, to the next level, until our love for others becomes closer to the "pure love of Christ." President Kimball has moved to a Celestial Level. A few years ago as I would listen to stories about how he always wanted to do *more,* how he was always LENGTHENING HIS STRIDE, I wondered why he didn't take a rest. I thought surely he must feel good about himself and his love for the Lord. He could relax here and there. Now I understand that feeling good about ourselves is a terrestrial level. President Kimball is always looking to love more, help more, give more with little thought of himself. That sounds exactly like the Savior to me!

It is an eternal principle that when you build and raise others, you build and raise yourself. Isn't that what Father and the Savior are doing for us right now? It takes a powerful force called LOVE.

There must have been a heavenly gathering the morning the Savior died. And since we were yet unborn, you and I must have been there. Contemplate that we were there. We saw the last supper, the trial and mockery, the suffering in Gethsemane. Imagine ourselves witnessing the beatings and humiliation of a brother whom we had just hugged goodbye thirty-three years earlier. And finally seeing Him hang and suffer on the cross, we knelt and wept together.

There is no way to imagine all that without realizing the impact of the moment. We knew! We knew what it all meant. And we were grateful. Don't you think we were grateful? Don't you think we might have made a similar covenant as did His disciples? That when it was our turn, when it was time for us to come, we would live our lives so His would not have been in vain. We *would* love others, as He loves us!

"The withholding of love is the negation of the spirit of Christ, the proof that we never knew him, that for us he lived in vain. It means that he suggested nothing in all our thoughts that he inspired nothing in all our lives, . . .'' (Marion D. Hanks, *Gift of Self*)

We *knew* of His great love for us. WE *KNEW* HIM then. Do we know Him now?

Chapter  Five

Rise Up And Never Be The Same Again

"I have yearned to be honorable all of my life, while I have continued to do unworthy things."
—*Dimitri Karamzov*

It isn't what you have been in the past or what you are at this very moment; it is what you may become that is important.

The Lord has given us the foundation upon which we may build better lives. First is the personal quest for perfection. We will achieve this line upon line, precept upon precept. With each new insight we will gain greater self-vision.

Through faith and hope we will constantly improve, overcome faults and weaknesses, learn to deal with others, and search for enriching opportunities. We must remember, perfection is a process, not an event.

The second part of that foundation is that we must give love and service for others throughout all our lives. Developing charity will allow us to develop those God-like qualities we desire so much. These are the foundations which our Lord has given us to become more righteous women.

To be a righteous woman is a glorious thing in any age. To be a righteous woman during the winding up scenes on this earth before the Second Coming of our Savior is an *especially noble calling*. The righteous woman's strength and influence today can be ten-fold what it might be in more tranquil times. (Spencer W. Kimball, *My Beloved Sisters,* page 17, emphasis added)

We have some tight places to go before the Lord is through with this Church and with us. But He has given us all the tools and keys to use to build a better life. And we have *inherited the power* to be able to use them and do it. If you will study them, ponder them, listen to them, use them, the promise is "the gates of Hell shall not prevail against you; yea and the Lord God will disperse the powers of darkness from before you, and cause the heavens to shake for your good and his name's glory." (*Doctrine and Covenants* 21:6) He promised.

The Lord needs you. He cannot get the work done without you. Satan knows it, so he whispers that you are not able, or capable, or worthy. What can be accomplished by a woman who doesn't feel capable or worthy? The Lord needs women who are valiant and can stand up and be counted, who use the spirit and *power within* them to battle Satan and choose the right direction. Women like that will not wallow in depression, frustration, or fear.

It is while you are standing undecided, uncommitted that you will be vulnerable to Satan and every life-threatening negative thought. It is taking a stand and making a choice to take charge of your life that will give you access to your powers within. It will be *speaking, acting,* and *thinking* like a potential God that will carry you to Godhood. If you don't make that choice now, this very hour, you will hide from the presence of God.

"For our *words* will condemn us, yea, all our *works* will condemn us; we shall not be found spotless; and our *thoughts* will also condemn us; and in this awful state we shall not dare to look up to our God; and we would fain be glad if we could command the rocks and the mountains to fall upon us to hide us from his presence." (Alma 12:14)

Faith, hope, and charity are spiritual gifts. If we are to gain these gifts, we must SEEK them. The Lord expects us to be anxiously engaged in seeking the best He has to give us, "Seek ye earnestly the best gifts." (*Doctrine and Covenants* 46:8) "Behold, thou hast a gift, or thou shalt have a gift if thou wilt desire of me in faith." (*Doctrine and Covenants* 11:10)

In seeking these gifts we must remember another gift we have been given, the gift of the Holy Ghost. He is the vehicle by which you may travel from one level to another, until you eventually arrive at the very gates of Godhood. He is a comforter, a companion, a healer, a teacher, a guardian, and a counselor. He is a friend! He will encourage you and inspire you all along the way. He will help you take that first step. If you will just seek Him, live to be worthy of Him by *striving* to obey the commandments, if you will watch and listen, He will be there.

I had my first experience with the Holy Ghost when I was seven years old. I was baptized on my eighth birthday, May 1, and my testimony came a few months prior to that, so this must have occurred in the winter—January or February of 1954.

My mother had joined the Church about a year and a half prior to this time, with my father following her on Valentine's Day, 1953. The gospel had changed their lives, so indirectly it had changed mine. But, I continually asked my mother, "How do you *KNOW* for sure it's true?" She taught me the principle of the Holy Ghost and her experiences of a burning in her heart. She was so convinced the Church was true that I thought it had to be; at seven years old my mother always knew the right answers. But I desired that burning in my heart; I desired to know for myself.

Primary was after school, I think on Thursday. Our class met on the stage behind the drawn curtains. It was cold back there; I remember pulling my sweater around me. Our class was preparing us for baptism, and the discussion that day had something to do with that. But the conversation turned to the *Book of Mormon*, and the thought went through my mind, "How do I know the *Book of Mormon* is true?" And then came the burning in my heart—and I knew.

When, a few months later, I went down into the waters of baptism, I knew I was joining the Lord's church.

I remember the white dress Mother made me. We were going to be sealed as a family in the Mesa temple later in the month, and she had made us girls matching temple dresses. She finished mine early so I could also be baptized in it. As I walked down into that warm water, and my dad held out his brown hands to escort me, my heart pounded. I pushed the little dress down in the water with Dad's help. He clasped my arm, and I his, and then I heard the words that were music to my ears: "Anita Rodriguez, having been commissioned of Jesus Christ, I baptize you in the name of the Father and of the Son and of the Holy Ghost, Amen."

As I came up out of the water, a warm glow seemed to permeate my soul, and I felt a renewing of my body. Someone said, "Anita, you are glowing," and in my soul I felt it, even the burning in my heart.

At age eight I lacked the maturity and vocabulary to express that event as I can now. The time, the years, the words have all changed—but the heart and those feelings have not. From the heart and mind of an innocent and tender eight-year-old child to that of a thirty-six-year-old woman—the Holy Ghost is real, positive, and still my friend.

I know this gospel is true. I know it. This gospel, this foundation contains all you need to know or do to regain or renew self-expectation, self-vision, and self-esteem. It is the truth, and I tell you that and bear witness in the Name of Jesus Christ.

The most unique feature about the Church of Jesus Christ of Latter-day Saints is that it is governed by Jesus Christ Himself through the promptings and direction of the Holy Ghost. Joseph Smith taught that the Holy Ghost has a *sanctifying and cleansing influence* upon the souls of men and is the source of *spiritual gifts and health.* Parley P. Pratt wrote that the Holy Ghost "invigorates all the faculties of the physical and intellectual man. It strengthens, and gives tone to the nerves. In short, it is, as it were, marrow to the bone, joy to the heart, light to the eyes, music to the ears, and life to the whole being." (*Key to Theology,* page 101)

The great and mighty prophet Enoch began his service to the Lord with a terrible self-image. And yet later he delivered such powerful sermons that no man dared to lay hands on him. Mountains and rivers moved their course for him. He taught his people by pure example, and he inspired them to become a righteous and unified city. So effective was his influence and love that eventually he and his entire city were lifted up, "for God received it up into his own bosom." (Moses 7:69) Enoch's companion was the Holy Ghost.

> And when Enoch had heard these words, he bowed himself to the earth, before the Lord, and spake before the Lord, saying: Why is it that I have found favor in thy sight, and am but a lad, and all the people hate me; for I am slow of speech; wherefore am I thy servant?
>
> And the Lord said unto Enoch: Go forth and do as I have commanded thee, and no man shall pierce thee. Open thy mouth, and it shall be filled, and I will give thee utterance, for all flesh is in my hands, and I will do as seemeth me good.
>
> Say unto this people: Choose ye this day, to serve the Lord God who made you.
>
> Behold *my Spirit* is upon you, . . . (Moses 6:31-34)

The Holy Ghost will help to quicken your mind as you commit to all the principles. He will help deliver you to the door of Self-Esteem. You must open the door and go in.

"If you live up to these principles . . . if you live up to your privileges, the angels cannot be restrained from being your associates." (Joseph Smith, Instructions to Women)

Someone once said, *"If you could catch the vision of the woman God intended for you to become, you would rise up and never be the same again!"* You *can* catch that vision. A little bit every day of your life. It is up to you. It doesn't matter who we are or where we are today. It is what we can become that excites me! When you started reading this book, you left your mortal roles in the other room. From cover to cover we are not wives, single women, mothers, young or old. We are simply WOMEN, DAUGHTERS, SISTERS.

At BYU Women's Week 1981, during his keynote address, President Jeffrey Holland called a young girl out of the audience:

What is your name?

Mary.

You are pretty young to be to this conference, aren't you?

Yes.

Are you sloughing school?

Sort of.

Do your parents know you are here?

Yes.

Do you have any brothers?

Yes.

Do you have any sisters?

No.

You are the only girl in your family?

Yes.

The *only* girl?

Yes.

Are you proud to be a girl?

Yes.

Do you think your parents are proud you're a girl?

Yes.

Do you think your dad loves you?

Yes.

Do you think he wants every righteous thing in this world
    for you?

Yes.

Does he dream about you and pray about you and love
    you with all his heart?

Yes.

Who is your dad?

You are.

My friends, this is Mary Alice Holland. She is our only daughter. She is also the light of her dad's life. Do I dream about her and pray about her and love her with all my heart? No one who is not the father of a daughter will ever know how much I dream about her and pray about her and love her with all my heart.

Do I want her to be happy? Do I want her to grow? Do I want her to be, in righteousness, everything in time or eternity she possibly, humanly, divinely can be? What foolish questions! This is bone of my bone, flesh of my flesh! This is my daughter! Of course, I want it! Do I want her disappointed or disillusioned or discriminated against? I want her happy, fulfilled, and blossoming into all that God intended her to be and discussed with her a long time ago. I want her to have strong family bonds in time and eternity, and I want her to be a queen, a priestess unto the Most High. (*Ye Are Free To Choose*)

Don't you think that is just exactly how Father in Heaven feels about you? Could He not have been having that conversation with you?

And then, could He not have turned to all of us and said the rest of President Holland's words:

The gospel of Jesus Christ gives her the one chance she has. Help her with her choices. She's eleven today. Tomorrow she is seventeen. The day after tomorrow she is gone away to start a life and family of her own. Then she is in your hands—you who will be her teachers, her guides, her friends. She already stands on the border of womanhood, that unique, mysterious sisterhood from which I and all other men are forever excluded. Soon she will fully be your sister. And she will always be my daughter.

We are fully sisters, you and I, and Father wants us home. He wants us to be teachers, guides, and friends to one another. He and Mother want us to serve and love one another. But They can't force us. They can't shape our lives. We must shape our own. We must discover and mold our own destiny. And your destiny, where does it lie?

From a sister, recently remarried after eleven years of being divorced:

When I was in the singles program, I would always grit my teeth when single women would wring their hands and lament: 'Yeah, Jan, but things seem to work out so well for you, so smooth for you.' You bet they worked out because I programmed them that way. For 11 years I raised the children, ran the home, held a full-time job, a regional calling, stake calling, two ward callings—and I loved every minute of it. I really hated to give it up and get married! I changed the things that I could, and adjusted to the things I couldn't change—and then—I turned my world into the happiest world I could. And it was a good world. And now, here I am again, with all kinds of challenging packages in front of me. Now some of the single women say to me: 'Yeah, Jan, you've been so lucky that things have worked out so well for you.' Things work out for me, because I program them to work out well. I can never remember one time in my life that I could honestly say that I was lonely or that I had nothing to do. And I can also say that I have had no experience in my lifetime—positive or negative—that I would have avoided had I the opportunity to do so. There have been some incredibly painful ones, but I'm still glad I went through them. I can even find positive aspects of the painful ones. . .

I have met so many women in the singles program who have such a great potential to show the tremendous strength they have within themselves. I'm thinking of one in particular, a beautiful woman with a couple of kids, divorced, skilled in the secretarial field, active in the Church, but she refuses to attend many singles activities because: 'There's nothing in it for me—no men, no fun, no future, etc.' I have yet to see a woman who is totally in service to others, very involved in callings, spiritually in tune, socially active with her church peers, wallowing in self-pity. How would she find the time? In my sixty-six years of good living, I wouldn't trade one chapter. It would be fantastic if every woman could experience all the things that I have experienced. I could probably have handled some of those chapters with a little more sophistication, with a little more sensitivity toward others, reshuffled some priorities at certain stages of my life—but trade any of those chapters in for someone else's—no way!

Your destiny lies within you, within the very thoughts with which you live each day. Your destiny lies in the pain and joy of bittersweet trials. Your destiny lies in the pure love of Christ. YOU are your destiny.

You will reach it, sisters. You will! If you will but commit to do it. And as you move forward in your commitment, as you move forward in faith, hope, and charity, as you begin to move mountains of fear, and doubt, and jealousy, you will catch a vision of the woman that God intends for you to become! The woman that you and He talked about before you left Home.

Mortality will not deal us equal amounts of love and fame or fortune. Mortality is not fair to everyone; eternity will be. But there is one thing we all can give back squarely, fairly, and equally. We can leave this world a better place than what we found it. Even if it is just our space around us, we can leave a sermon of our life—a sermon that says, "I know who I am. I know who I can become. I am going to where she is!"

All summer long I have struggled to write this book, yet nothing came. We even went back to the ocean where the first one was written, but I felt nothing. One afternoon Steve took the children away so I could be alone. When they came home four hours later, only one page was written. I ended up throwing that away.

The spirit wasn't there. I wanted that same *feeling* I had in writing the other books. I didn't have anything to say.

Two weeks ago I woke up on a Saturday morning and knew that was the day! Within an hour I had every chapter title, I had an outline, and it was perfectly clear how the gospel helps us conquer our doubts, fears, and jealousies. By the end of the day several pages were written. And for two weeks I have written every spare moment. It has been as if I were spending intimate, personal moments with you—*individually.* I have missed you; it is so great to visit again. It is my desire that you read this book with the spirit in which it was written—that you read and re-read it. And as you read, that you underline and write your thoughts in the margins. I cannot imagine reading a book without a pen in hand. In fact, I love to read books belonging to someone who has underlined. You get in touch with how they think and feel. Your spirit communicates with theirs. Another great lesson about underlining is that when you do re-read a book, you find how much progress you are making. You come to things that you underlined long ago that once mattered, once applied to you but no longer seem necessary. You can see your growth as you return and reevaluate. It is my hope that you will return and visit again and again with me in this book. That together we can help one another reach our goals. You are blessing my life. You inspire me! I look to you for strength, example, and unity of sisterhood and womanhood. It is true what President Kimball said about the strength of righteous women being an influence to the world in the last days. I feel that spirit resting on the land. I feel that in you. I love you for that.

I also ask you to forgive me of my weaknesses. Someone once asked me how it felt to write a book and sign my name on the front page. I told her that every sin, every weakness, everything I've done that has offended others passes in front of my mind. I ask you to forgive me of imperfections and no discredit these gospel principles because of the weak areas in my life. They work! They are working for me. As an ordinary mortal woman, who feels the same as you, who feels pain and joy the same as you, if they are *working* for me, they will work for you.

You, noble daughter of God, you were born to bless the lives of others. I am convinced of everything I have read or spiritually felt, that the Lord saved the best for last. The best of all He has. Women who could reach deep within themselves and find *power*, real power to fight the physical, spiritual, and emotional battles of the last days. Women who would lead and influence the world. Women who would do so by *cherishing* and *using* their differences, not to serve themselves, but to serve their God. You are those women; the world is looking to you. And the Lord is counting on you. You wouldn't be here if He didn't *expect* you to be able to do it!

The whole Church must know that on President Kimball's desk is a little sign that says "DO IT NOW." Do it now! That is the secret of commitment. That is the secret of keeping a house clean, or how to stop smoking, or losing weight, or altering negative thoughts. It is the secret to any success.

So many of us never make it because after having been motivated, inspired, enthused, we say, "I feel so great! I'll change! I'll start in the morning!"

And the morning never comes.

Do it now! I hope you can feel the sisterhood I feel. That "mysterious sisterhood" isn't so mysterious. I am convinced that we all knew one another well when we were Home. We taught one another.

We agreed to help one another, to serve one another, to love one another. We knew what it would mean to become like our Heavenly Parents. We knew what a Celestial Level would mean. We have got to come from that terrestrial level of feeling good about our accomplishments to that Celestial level of loving and wanting to serve more!

We will get there, line upon line, precept upon precept, *together.* We will get there because we will catch the vision of the Woman God intends for us to become. We know who we are.

Commit to it. Not this day, not this hour, but this very moment . . .

Rise up . . .

AND NEVER BE THE SAME AGAIN!